PRESENTED TO

HEIDI OTTO

By
Spring Lake Park Baptist Church
Graduate Sunday, June 5, 2005

i am not but i know
I AM

i am not
but i know
I AM

L O U I E   G I G L I O
[iamnot]

Multnomah® Publishers *Sisters, Oregon*

I AM NOT BUT I KNOW I AM
published by Multnomah Publishers, Inc.

© 2005 by Louie Giglio
International Standard Book Number: 1-59052-275-3

Cover design by benji peck for b posi+ive studios
Cover image by Getty Images/Angela Wyant

Unless otherwise indicated, Scripture quotations are from:
The Holy Bible, New International Version
© 1973, 1984 by International Bible Society,
used by permission of Zondervan Publishing House
Other Scripture quotations are from:
New American Standard Bible (NASB)
© 1960, 1977 by the Lockman Foundation

The Holy Bible, *English Standard Version* (ESV)
© 2001 by Crossway Bibles, a division of Good News Publishers.
Used by permission. All rights reserved.

Multnomah is a trademark of Multnomah Publishers, Inc.,
and is registered in the U.S. Patent and Trademark Office.
The colophon is a trademark of Multnomah Publishers, Inc.

Printed in the United States of America

For information:
MULTNOMAH PUBLISHERS, INC.
POST OFFICE BOX 1720
SISTERS, OREGON 97759

Library of Congress Cataloging-in-Publication Data

Giglio, Louie.
    I am not but I know I Am / by Louie Giglio.
        p. cm.
    ISBN 1-59052-275-3
    1.   Spirituality.   I. Title.
    BV4501.3.G54 2005
    248—dc22

                                                          2005001608

05 06 07 08 09 10—10 9 8 7 6 5 4 3 2 1 0

For my mom—Martha Jeane Giglio—I love you.

contents

START here

Life is the tale of two stories—one finite and frail, the other eternal and enduring. The tiny one—the story of us—is as brief as the blink of an eye. Yet somehow our infatuation with our own little story—and our determination to make it as big as we possibly can—blinds us to the massive God Story that surrounds us on every side.

It's a little like me being shocked a few weeks ago by the reaction of two of New York City's finest as they motioned me over to their squad cars in the middle of my mid-morning run. The first officer's opening line (the exact wording of which, I'm sad to say, cannot be repeated here) led to the inexcusable reply,

"What does it look like I'm doing?"

I quickly realized I had said the wrong thing, especially to a New York cop. In a heartbeat my hands were on the hood of his car and threats of arrest were flying all over the place. I was startled and unnerved, and though it was now too late, my mouth was shut. Unless asked, I wasn't saying another word, especially a sarcastic one.

To make matters worse, all I could produce in the way of identification was a hotel key card—one of those fancy new ones that looks cool but doesn't even contain the name and address of the hotel. The whole scene was going down-hill fast…

Things had started off innocently enough that morning as I headed out the door of our midtown-Manhattan hotel and began plodding down the sidewalk toward the East River about eight blocks away. But before I was two or three blocks away it started to rain. First it was just annoying—an inter-mittent spitting kind of rain. Then the wind picked up and a steady, chilling downpour started making things miserable. Assessing the situation, I determined I was too far from the hotel to make turning back a sensible option, so I kept running north along the river, pressing on in the driving rain.

I don't know what kind of shape you're in, but when I run I think more about survival than scenery. And when I'm running in a cold downpour, I barely think at all. I certainly don't look around to read a lot of the signs. Thus, I wasn't paying much attention when suddenly my path was blocked by a chain-link fence. It stretched from the river-bank on my right to a concrete lane divider that had been following me on my left. Once again I considered my options. Retracing my steps still didn't make sense. What made sense was getting out of the rain. So without thinking I hopped over the lane divider and headed for the shelter of an overpass I now noticed across the way.

Quickly the overpass turned into an elevated roadway, so I could keep running under cover. I continued north, not really noticing that the lane to my right at some point became two lanes of traffic, and then three. After another mile or so, all three lanes of traffic were moving slower than I was and a driver in one of the cars shouted something in my direction. But in the rain and traffic, I couldn't quite make out her words and was trying to ignore her anyway. Then the overpass drifted away to the left and I was once again exposed to the rain.

Soon I noticed the lower levels of the United Nations buildings on my far left, and nearer and just ahead two police cars parked on a wide concrete median. A single officer sat in each car, their eyes meeting mine as each step I ran drew us closer. Everything seemed to be fine, until my forward progress was interrupted by the piercing "*blurp*" of one of the officer's sirens and the intense motion of his hand directing me to approach his car.

It was at that moment I realized for the first time I was running down the middle of the FDR, a six-lane expressway that snakes along the eastside shoreline of Manhattan. No wonder the officer's first question when I finally splashed to a stop in front of his car was incredulous and unprintable.

How can you run down the middle of a New York freeway and not know it? I think the same way you can live your entire life completely oblivious to the grand story of the Creator of the universe that is unfolding all around you. The same way you can spend your days making so much of someone as small and transient as you or me, and so little of someone as glorious and eternal as God.

That's why this book is not about you and making your story better, but about waking up to the infinitely bigger God Story happening all around you, and God's invitation to you to join Him in it. It's about looking up to see that there's a story that has been going on long before you arrived on the planet and one that will go on long after you're gone. God is the central character of this story and of this book. He commands center stage in existence, Creation, time, life, history, redemption, and eternity.

I'm not trying to put you down or imply that you don't matter. Nor am I saying that you are absent from the grand Story of God. In fact, just the opposite. Amazingly, you appear on every page, existing in God's thoughts long before this world was made. I'm simply stating the obvious—that

THE STORY ALREADY HAS A STAR, AND THE STAR IS NOT YOU OR ME.

And here's why it matters—if we don't get the two stories straight, everything else in our lives will be out of sync. We'll spend our days trying to hijack the Story of God, turning it into the story of us. Inverting reality, we'll live every day as though life is all about you and me. We'll live as though life is our one-act play and history *our* story—as though Creation is our habitation alone, existence our playground, and God our servant (that is, if we decide we need Him at all). We will throw every ounce of our energy into the fragmented and fleeting story of us. Calling the shots ourselves, me-centered thinking will dictate every move we make and how we feel.

And in the end—when the last clap is clapped for our tiny tale—our story will fade to black, a pitiful return on our one-shot chance called "life on earth."

About thirty minutes into my ordeal with the officers, the situation lightened a bit as I realized the worst that was going to happen to me was a ticket for jaywalking, something I certainly deserved. As we were waiting for my life's history to appear on the squad car's computer, the nicer of the two cops asked within earshot of the other, "So what do you do for a living, anyway?"

Hmmm.

Opting for the short answer, I said, "I'm a pastor." Two sets of eyebrows rose.

"A pastor! What kind of pastor are *you*?"

I think he was looking for the name of a denomination, but I replied, "I'm a Christian."

"Oh, yeah? Well what are you doing in New York?"

"I'm here to speak to a group of college students tonight out in Queens."

"So, what are you going to tell them?"

For a split second time stood still. And then I told him, "I'm going to remind them that life is short and our time on earth is really brief," I said. "That's why we have to make sure our lives count for the stuff that lasts forever."

That's what I want to do in these pages, too. Lead you to a fresh awareness of the six-lane-wide-freeway-sized

God Story that you and I are running down the middle of every day.

It's a place that requires a constant choice. We can choose to cling to *starring* roles in the little-bitty stories of us, or we can exchange our fleeting moment in the spotlight for a supporting role in the eternally beautiful epic that is the Story of God.

Think of it as trading up. Abandoning the former and embracing the latter will allow our little lives to be filled with the wonder of God as we live for His fame and the unending applause of His name. And joining our small stories to His will give us what we all want most in life anyway: the assurance that our brief moments on earth count for something in a story that never ends.

LOOK up

Given the unusual

August heat, it's remarkably cool in here. And quiet.

At least it was until now.

A noisy Italian family has just clamored past me down the aisle, oblivious to the stillness.

From where I'm sitting, it looks like Grandma, her favorite (perhaps only) son, his wife, and their three kids.

They all seem instantly impressed, even the daughter, who is now fighting through her outer shell of teen-cool to pull the headphones out of her ears. As she looks up, her mouth is wide open, her lips mouthing *W-o-w!* in slow motion for no one in particular to hear.

A rapid flurry of conversation is being exchanged between them, spearheaded by the dad whose voice is nearing full volume. Making out the word *magnifico,* I think he just offered for the family's consideration, "isn't this place magnificent?"

Everyone except the littlest one nods, especially Grams, who seems to be genuinely awestruck by what she sees, and maybe equally moved that she is seeing it with the people she loves most. She looks to be close to seventy. A small, roundish woman with a gentle smile and still sparkling eyes.

Dad, as you might expect, has the tourist look—sandals (with dark socks, of course), zip-off cargo pants, sunglasses perched atop a closely shaved head, and the can't-leave-home-without-it fanny pack. He's holding an open brochure which rattles in the air as he gestures wildly.

Then there's Mom—all classic Italian glam with her designer jeans, high heels and hip shades.

Isabella, the teen daughter (yes, I know her name now, as do all those within fifty feet of her dad) is trying her best to have a good time without appearing to be overly "into" the family outing. Her jeans are ragged out and about four inches too long, hiding what I think are Birkenstocks underneath. A pink backpack follows her every move, as does the attached snowboard-shaped key chain that swings from side to side. Fortunately for her younger teen brother, the key chain is at just the right height for him to demonstrate his kung-fu skills with his foot, which he does repeatedly on the way down the aisle.

And then there's little Paulie. At maybe five or six, he must be the darling of the clan. Every other second his name echoes off the walls, being constantly called by father, mother, brother, sister, and grandma. But Paulie is zoned out in Nintendo land, and I'm pretty sure he doesn't hear a thing. He's simply following along with a child's sixth sense, never taking his eyes off the video images dancing on the screen of the game player that's firmly in his grip.

Little does he know, he's in a place that bears his name.

Enormous and ancient, St Paul's Cathedral is one of the world's most amazing structures, completed more than three hundred years ago in an era when the very act of coming to worship caused you to look up in awe and wonder.

For an hour or so a steady stream of reverent (and not so reverent) onlookers have come by. A multitude of faces and cultures. A tour group of about sixty. A few dozen school kids with British accents. Couples. Loners. Families like my Italian family. And you know what? They've all been doing exactly the same thing—craning their necks and looking high above. For good reason—the ceiling looms nine stories above, giving way to the world's second largest vaulted dome, a cavernous opening spanning more than a hundred feet—a jaw-dropping ring of open wonder rising still higher overhead.

To say this place is huge is a massive understatement. It's almost two football fields long, the dome alone weighs sixty-five thousand tons, and the cross that adorns its outer shell rises 365 feet above London's Ludgate Hill, the spot of earth that has been home to a church building since 1087.

But St. Paul's is lifting my heart and my head toward something even bigger, something higher, Someone more. Sure, Christopher Wren's architectural masterpiece is a testimony to the ingenuity, skill, and determination of man. But even in its grandeur, St. Paul's fails to reach near heaven, and its exterior is often shrouded by scaffolding and tarps as fatigue-fighters and renovators wage a continuing battle against the corrosive powers of time. And though the cathedral miraculously survived the relentless bombings of World War II, St. Paul's will not stand forever. Yet the God this building speaks of will, a fact that seems more real to me than ever as I gaze up from my pew.

Sitting here, I'm feeling pretty small.

Granted, we shouldn't need massive buildings to evoke an awareness of grandeur in us, especially given the cathedral of earth and sky we call home. Besides, the real church is those of us who believe—a spirit-infused marvel of God's constructive genius—and not the lifeless fortress of stone that encompasses me now. Just the same, this place is special, and by simply being here I'm shrinking on the inside, listening to the constant echo that declares both bigness and smallness, His and mine.

Now a young girl is whispering excitedly to her friend, "This is where Princess Di got married!" Granted these walls have witnessed their fair share of pomp and pageantry, but somehow pop culture is lost on me in this moment. St. Paul's speaks of more than history. This place is a window to eternity. It's as if the building is doing in this moment just what it was designed to do—whispering softly,

"GOD IS BIG. REALLY, REALLY BIG."

And, I am not.

Sitting here, I feel so small—and small feels surprisingly good. So good I begin to wonder why it's so surprising that feeling small feels so good.

The truth is, feeling small may not be so bad if in recognizing our smallness we come to realize the wonder of God—a God who is beyond our ability to fully describe or imagine, yet someone we are privileged to know, love, and embrace. Looking up from our tiny estate we are faced with the supremacy of a God who not only is fully capable of running the entire cosmos today—a task that doesn't tax Him in the slightest—but of sustaining the affairs of our lives as well.

You would think getting a glimpse of God's true size would have us happily lining up to embrace our little-bitty lives, especially given we are loved so dearly by the One who gives them to us in the first place. But then again, human history is not exactly the record of man's unquenchable quest for smallness. More accurately, our history is a stark reminder of our insatiable quest to make our names, our fortunes, our fame, and our kingdom as vast and enduring as possible.

Unfortunately, such a quest is an exhausting proposition. For one thing, none of us seems to know when "big" is big enough, leading us up a dizzying and deceptive staircase that promises contentment while constantly beckoning us one rung higher to an "even more." But somehow more is never quite enough and the climb continues. Even more exhausting, our preoccupation with ourselves puts us at odds with God Himself, given that any attempt to pump up our names is, in effect, an attempt to push Him from the center and steal His glory—a quest as tiring and futile as trying to extinguish the sun with an eye dropper.

So if you're at a place in life where weariness and strain are more commonplace than rest and wonder, this book has found you at just the right time. God knows you better than you know yourself. He knows just how small and frail you are. He knows you're just one person, and a tiny one at that. He knows all the things that you are not—and He made you that way for a purpose. That's why He has never asked you to be more than you are—little you with a great big God.

But God also is in touch with just how potent He is, desiring to do huge, God-sized things through you if you're ready to abandon the path of making more of self and embrace the miracle of being small, yet knowing His name.

It all starts when you look up.

It's been a few minutes, but that's exactly what my Italian friends are still doing. While they're looking up, I'm wondering if they've ever seen a glimpse of heaven, or if they know they have been invited to know God intimately and join His story.

I can't help thinking about Isabella. Obviously, I don't know her, but I gravitate toward her because she looks a lot like the students that our ministry seeks to lead. It may just be me, but I don't think there are too many sixteen year olds who are living in a greater story, embracing each day as if the purpose of life is a whole lot bigger than them. Sure that's a generalization (There are a lot of passionate, Christ-following teens out there!), but so many teenagers are all about me and mine—my hair, my fashion, my friends, my approval and acceptance by others, my being in the right place at the right time with the right people. Funny, they're a lot like us, just not mature enough to manage their selfishness as well as some of us older folks do. I really want Isabella to wake up to the bigger story because most of her life is ahead of her, and she brings a sense of youthful wonder to the table that all of us in the story really need.

Then there's little Paulie. Oh boy. How can he *not* think life is all about him? After all, isn't that what we are saying a lot of the time to kids these days from the second they're born? But what they really need to hear at birth is, "We love you so much, and want you to know we are really excited you are here. Welcome to the story that is already in progress!"

What about Dad? Chances are, he's a lot like me in the sense that a lot of the time he thinks he is at the helm of his life. I can see him on the phone, doing the deal, managing the enterprise. He thinks it's all in his hands—the business, the relationships, the equity, the direction, and the future. He loves his family, but he's married to his work. He believes in God, but in the daily flow of life he acts like he doesn't need Him at all. He thinks he's generous, yet he keeps shoving his stuff into a bigger pile. He thinks he has it all together, but the foundation is a lot shakier than he knows. At the end of the day, he's going to be dumbfounded when he finds out just how tiny he really is, and discovers that God gave him life and breath and everything in between so that he would have something to contribute to the massive God-mission that has no end.

As for Mom, I'm guessing that her story on most days is whatever is on the other end of the phone, whatever the latest raging topic is between her friends. It's like somehow she's telling me something without saying a word—"My kids have the right stuff, I have the right stuff, we live in the right neighborhood, attend the right schools, do mass at the right church, vacation in the right places...." I doubt she knows where she put the story down, that is if she ever picked it up in the first place. I wonder if she knows that God invented the stuff in Botox and that He loves her with or without it. I'm sitting wondering if her heart is shrinking with the dying story of her and hers, wondering if she's ever known the rush of hearing Him call her by name.

Oh yeah, I almost overlooked the middle boy. But I

guess it's not the first time. He's not the anointed—daddy's little girl—or the precious little baby boy. Everyone is always looking out for Paulie, even him. Oops. I'm not talking about the middle son, am I? He's pretty determined he's going to make something in life about him. But I hope he doesn't.

And we close with sweet little Grandma. At the family table she probably never sits down—always serving, always moving, always making sure everyone else has what they want. One minute she's making sure the lasagna is served piping hot, and the next that Paulie gets his cobbler with just a little scoop of ice cream on a different plate because he doesn't like it when the cobbler and the ice cream touch each other. Dad wants coffee with milk. Isabella doesn't like the apple cobbler, so there is a small cherry one for her. No wonder Grandma never sits!

My first inclination is to just give her a hug and say thank you, thinking that she is living such a bigger story, not settling for a tiny one that is all about her. But just then it hits me that sin is deceptively strong and that pride has many faces.

I want to tell Grams that it's okay for her to sit and eat. I'm presuming Grandpa has already gone and I'm guessing she wonders a lot about where he is and if she'll ever see him again. Eternity is on her mind a lot, as it should be.

I WANT TO TELL HER THERE'S A BIG, HUGE, HOLY GOD ON THE OTHER SIDE WAITING FOR HER.

And encourage her that even though she will be completely floored by His glory when she sees Him, she doesn't have to be afraid. I want to tell her about the love of God and the gift of His Son.

You think Grandma's too old for all this tiny story/huge story stuff to matter?

I don't. If I could, I'd remind her that Moses was a little older than she is now when he got a surprising invitation to look up, trade up...and step into an incredible role in the great Story of God.

DIVINE invitation

God is always looking for ordinary people to play significant roles in His unfolding story.

And, given that He is God and supremely confident in Himself, He is free to choose the least among us—the slowest, the lesser-known, the last, the smallest, the poorest—to accomplish amazing, God-sized stuff. While as humans we try to partner with the brightest and most powerful, God is simply looking for people who are willing to take Him at

His word—those confident that with Him in the equation everything is possible.

So try to put yourself in God's shoes for a minute. Your people are enslaved in Egypt, toiling day and night building monuments to the fame and greatness of the Pharaohs. Yet you have a redemption plan, a deliverance mission, and you're looking for a spokesman to take your agenda to the most powerful man in the most powerful empire on the planet, demanding that he let your people go free. Who are you going to choose to lead Israel out of bondage? What criteria are you going to use to narrow the field of candidates? How will you train the person you choose to lead? How will you ensure the success of the mission?

Well, you probably wouldn't choose a stuttering shepherd with wilting self-esteem—an aging man on the downslope of life who for years had been on the run from the mighty Pharaoh after killing one of his slave drivers back in Egypt. Would you? But that's exactly who God chose—just the guy He invited to take the helm in this chapter of His unfolding story.

I'm guessing you probably know what happened. When Moses looked up, a nearby bush was on fire. But what was really strange was the fact that the bush continued to burn without being consumed. Intrigued, Moses stopped to investigate, and when he moved in for a closer look a voice thundered out of the flames,

"MOSES, MOSES."

Moses stopped in his tracks.
God had found His man.

Not that finding Moses was all that difficult for God. He didn't have to do a Google search. He knew exactly where to find him. For even though Moses was on the "backside of nowhere," the nowhere he was on the backside of was a place called Mt. Horeb—a name which means the mountain of God. Moses probably thought he was alone with the flock for another dusty day, stranded in the wilderness, just counting the days in the closing chapters of his life. Little did he know that he was tending his sheep in God's neighborhood, or that he was about to be invited to play a major role in God's deliverance plan.

In what would turn out to be a very prophetic reply, Moses answered, "Here I am."

That's when Moses' world turned upside down. "Take off your sandals, Moses, and don't come any closer," God exclaimed. "You are on holy ground."

I doubt Moses needed a second admonition. Instantly he ripped the sandals from his feet and buried his face in his hands.

Now that He had Moses' undivided attention, God laid out His plan. "I have indeed seen the misery of My people in Egypt. I have heard them crying out because of their slave drivers and I am concerned about their suffering. So I have come down to rescue them and bring them into a good and spacious land. The cry of the Israelites has reached Me and I have seen the way the Egyptians are oppressing them."

Did you notice all the first-person pronouns God is using to state His case? *I* have seen. *I* have heard. *I'm* concerned. *I'm* coming down. *I'm* going to do something.

God's mind was set. His plan was in motion. Failure was not an option. No insurmountable obstacle stood in His way. God had sized up Pharaoh, a man of unrivaled political and military power, and decided to use him as a pawn in His story. The redemption mission would go on as scheduled, Pharaoh's army notwithstanding, and a couple million people would journey through an arid desert wasteland to safely arrive in the land long ago promised to their forefathers. Mark it down. It was going to happen. God was confident that the Promised Land—the place He had chosen for Israel to dwell—was suitably perfect, even if presently inhabited by skilled warriors defending cities whose fortressed walls would intimidate any man (see the formidable list of "ites" in Exodus 3:8b). God wasn't deterred and He didn't need assistance. But He had chosen to use a man, a human mouthpiece—someone who would carry His message and lead His cause. That's when, for Moses, the conversation took an ominous turn.

Without taking a breath, God added,

"SO NOW, GO, I AM SENDING YOU TO PHARAOH TO BRING MY PEOPLE THE ISRAELITES OUT OF EGYPT."

What? All of a sudden the first-person God is going to do something amazing through someone else, someone small. Somehow the "I" and "Me" pronouns evaporate and Moses is left reeling in the wake of blatantly second-person marching orders: "Now you go."

Confused and overwhelmed, Moses blurts out, "Who am I, that I should go to Pharaoh and bring the Israelites out of Egypt?"

I think what was going through Moses' mind were the same kind of thoughts that have raced through yours and mine when we're called by God to do something that seems way beyond our abilities. *God, are You serious? Is this a joke? Have You mistaken me for somebody else? Surely You don't think I can pull this off, do You? Who, me? Do what?*

But look more closely at what God actually said to Moses.

When He said, "You go and bring them out," He wasn't thinking Moses was going to actually do the delivering. God wasn't counting on Moses' skill or power to break the chains of bondage that held His people captive. God was going to do all the work, He just wanted a leader with skin to speak on His behalf and lead the people to His promised destination. All along God was counting on Himself to pull the story off—not Moses. Definitely not Moses.

When God said, "You go," He was implying: "I am going to do this with or without you, Moses, but I've been searching for just the right partner, a regular guy who will believe that I am able to do exactly what I have said I will do. You just need to merge onto the highway of My agenda—My promised before, now happening, already in motion agenda—and watch Me go. Don't deviate from what I am saying. Trust Me. Follow Me without fear of any man. This is going to be amazing. Oh, and by the way, I could do it all by Myself, but I'm choosing to use a human vessel—a tangible, flesh and blood ambassador for the cause. And I am choosing you, Moses. So now you go!"

But those last two words were the only ones Moses heard.

"YOU GO!"

Immediately, the questions and doubts gushed out of his mouth, "A stuttering man like me? You want me to go to Pharaoh? How? He'll kill me!"

Interestingly, God didn't respond with a pep talk. He didn't send Moses to the Center for "You Can Do It" Training in an effort to boost his confidence. No, God doesn't waste any time—not one second—trying to pump Moses up for the task. He doesn't inflate Moses' self-esteem by filling him with a boatload of "Come on Moses, you can do this! I believe in you—you've just got to believe in yourself!" encouragement.

Instead, God answers Moses' "Who am I?" question with five life-shifting words as He simply affirms, "I will be with you."

When God invites us into His Story, assigning us various roles that are seemingly too big for us to carry out, His affirmation is always the same—I will be with you.[1] It's as if He was saying to Moses, "Don't worry about who you are, just focus on the reality that I'm going, too. And if I go with you, trust Me, everything's going to work out fine."

Bottom line: God and anybody else is an overwhelmingly powerful team.

By now, things were getting dicey for Moses, but he didn't fold up and run. After all, the bush was still a raging flame and a holy hush was hanging thick in the air. Barefoot and trembling, Moses somehow mustered the courage to ask God to produce some personal identification.

Honestly, who could blame him? It's not likely Moses was going to go charging into Egypt, instantly gaining the trust of the Israelites while striking fear into the heart of an iron-fisted dictator like Pharaoh. No, before that was going to happen, Moses knew he'd need a lot more information about the One who was sending him and who would be going with him.

"How will they know we had this conversation?" Moses likely stuttered. "They won't believe the burning bush thing even if I tell them and they won't be able to sense the 'otherness' of Your presence like I can right now. If they say, 'And just who was this God you were talking to out in the wilderness?' what will I tell them?"

Can you believe it? Moses is asking the God of all Creation to tell him His name.

It's important here to grasp the gravity of the situation. Of course, God already knew Moses' name (He had repeatedly called him by his first name at the outset of this exchange). But Moses didn't know His. Since the dawn of time, God had been referred to as Yahweh, meaning Most High God—a name so revered by the generations preceding Moses, they rarely even wrote it out in full (choosing instead to abbreviate it).

But that revered title was really more of a description than a personal name. No one knew God's personal name. And, as far as we know, no one had dared to ask.

You have to understand, it's not as though God was just a little higher and a little more holy than Moses, someone you'd just stroll up to and say, "Hey man, what's up?" No, we're talking about the Infinite One—the One whose voice alone causes worlds to be born and grown men to hide their faces—having a conversation with a little, frail, finite creature. A creature who wants to know if he can call almighty God by name.

God was in no way obligated to answer, yet without hesitation, He did. To this aging shepherd, God revealed His name, saying,

"I AM WHO I AM. TELL THEM, I AM SENT ME TO YOU."

What?

I'm pretty sure Moses didn't get it right away. In fact he was probably thinking, *That's what I'm asking You, God. You are, who?*

And the reply comes back, "*I AM* [long pause], that's who."

"Your name is *I AM?*"

"That's right, Moses, my name is *I AM WHO I AM*. My name is *I AM.*"

I wonder how long it took for God's name to register in Moses' brain...

It's an amazing name. In Hebrew the word for *I AM* is *Hayah*, the pronunciation of which originates deep down in the throat (think of the loud Karate expression here). *Hayah* carries with it the idea of the very breath of God.

In English the name I AM translates into the verb *to be*. Or simply *be*.

Therefore, God's name is *Be. I AM = I BE*. Not great grammar, I know, but powerful theology.

God knew it was imperative for Moses to know who He was—that He was *I AM*. *I AM* is the present tense, active form of the verb *to be*. As God's name, it declares that He is unchanging, constant, unending, always present, always God.

God was telling Moses:

I AM the center of everything.

I AM running the show.

I AM the same every day, forever.

I AM the owner of everything.

I AM the Lord.

I AM the Creator and Sustainer of life.

I Am the Savior.

I AM more than enough.

I AM inexhaustible and immeasurable.

I AM God.

In a heartbeat, Moses knew God's name—and something more. He finally knew his. For if God's name is *I AM*, Moses' name must be *I am not.*

I am not the center of everything.

I am not in control.

I am not the solution.

I am not all-powerful.

I am not calling the shots.

I am not the owner of anything.

I am not the Lord.

That's my name, too. And yours. *I am not.* Just try it under your breath, "My name is *I am not.*"

I am not running anything.

I am not the head of anything.

I am not in charge of anything.

I am not the maker.

I am not the savior.

I am not holding it all together.

I am not all-knowing.

I am not God.

Sure, people might call you Tommy or Eddie or Amanda or Juan or Michelle or Erin or Michael. But, let's face it, when you get right down to it, all of our names are *I am not.*

And God's name is still **I AM.**

While Moses was still reeling, God continued, "This is my name forever, the name by which I am to be remembered from generation to generation" (Exodus 3:15). In other words, God wanted Moses to know that not only would He remain the same, His name would endure to every generation that would inhabit earth—even to our generations, mine and yours.

I love this verse, because it puts us in the story. Oh, you may have just been calling Him God all these years—and, in fact, that's who He is. But He gladly told Moses His name is *I AM* [*BE*] and that's still His name today. Right now. Wherever and whoever you are.

God is big. We are not. He is calling the shots, directing the script, and determining the plot. We are not. And, what's really wild is that while He doesn't *need* any of us, He is *choosing* to include us, inviting us into the story that never ends.

Try to fathom it—little you and me invited into the massive and mysterious story of the great *I AM.*

Are you up for it?

LIGHT flies

Light flies.

If you don't believe me go outside tonight, crank up the family car, and try to race the beam streaming from the headlights to the end of the driveway. Light is fast—really fast—traveling at 186,000 miles per second. How fast is that? In the time it takes you to snap your fingers just once, a ray of light can circle the globe seven times. Like I said, light is quick.

Light has to be fast because the universe is so big. The warmth you feel on your face when you walk outside on a sunny afternoon is light that left the surface of the sun eight minutes ago. If you wanted to repeat the 93-million-mile journey and return to the sun (not a good idea given that the temperature at the sun's surface is ten thousand degrees Fahrenheit, and it would vaporize you long before your arrival), the trip would take you seventeen years flying nonstop, twenty-four hours a day, in our fastest jet.

I don't know about you, but a beam of light covering 93 million miles in eight minutes is pretty hard for me to comprehend. Much less the news that a team of astrophysicists recently discovered what is believed to be the farthest object from earth, a tiny galaxy that is 13 billion light years away.

If you want to put that distance in perspective, consider that a light year (how far light travels in 365 days) is equal to 5.88 trillion miles. If it helps, that number again is 5,880,000,000,000 miles. That's a lot of zeros, and frankly, a number too large to really mean anything of significance to most of us. We can fathom the inch, the yard, the meter and the mile. Most of us can get our heads around the fact that it's about 3,000 miles from Atlanta to L.A., a mile being four times around the track at the local high school football field, thus L.A. being 12,000 laps from Atlanta.

But how are we supposed to grasp the idea of something blazing through the universe at 186,000 miles a second, morning and night, for an entire year? A light year—who needs it? You're thinking, *Not me.*

Then again, astronomers—who work in an environment where miles and kilometers lose meaning—love and need the light year in their quest to map out the cosmological landscape around us.[2] Thus, the folks at the California Institute of Technology are fairly certain their newly discovered galaxy is 13,000,000,000 times 5,880,000,000,000 miles away. That qualifies it as the oldest visible light in all Creation, and the farthest thing from earth our eyes have ever seen. Actually, since a light year is more about time than distance, when we gaze at this most-distant-yet galaxy, we're looking at light that left there 13 billion years ago. That means that we're actually looking back across time, deep into the past.

But let's bring things closer to home—you know, *home,* our galactic neighborhood, the Milky Way. Our cozy little corner of space, the Milky Way Galaxy, is somewhere between 100,000 and 130,000 light years across. So to get from one end of our neighborhood to the other, all you have to do is zoom at 186,000 miles per second for 100,000 plus years. Our galaxy is home to hundreds of billions of stars, only one of which is our sun. Our solar system—whose star is the sun—is located about twenty-five thousand light years from the center of the Milky Way. And just as the planets in our solar system orbit the sun, so our sun and all of the other hundreds of billions of other stars in the Milky Way orbit around its center—a galactic revolution that takes our sun 250 million earth years to complete.

By way of a quick review:

We have no idea just how big the universe is, but it's so big we have to use a ruler that's 5.88 trillion miles long to measure stuff. The ruler is called a light year.

The farthest thing we have measured so far with the help of a mighty telescope (actually two telescopes, one in Hawaii and one in space, combining together and aided by the natural magnification provided by a massive cluster of galaxies) is 13 billion light years way.

Somewhere in the midst of it all is a spiral galaxy called the Milky Way, which is made up of hundreds of billions of stars.

One of those stars is our sun, rotating around the center of the Milky Way every 250 million years.

One of the planets circling our sun is Planet Earth.

And two of the more than six billion people on this planet are you and me.

Speaking of you and me, here we sit, reading these tiny

printed characters on this page. Along with you and me, there are over 6 billion other humans dotting this minute ball we call earth (our planet is a mere 8,000 miles in diameter), which is orbiting an average star in a tiny solar system that's hovering on the outskirts of the Milky Way, one of billions of galaxies in the known universe, the size of which exponentially expands our latest measurements every time we manage to build a more powerful telescope.

A shrinking feeling is coming over me—like that day in St. Paul's—and I'm starting to clue in on the fact that I have no idea how small I really am.

OR HOW BIG GOD TRULY IS.

Light flies, yet the universe that so easily blows our minds is nothing more than a speck to God. Scripture tells us that, "By the word of the LORD the heavens were made, their starry host by the breath of His mouth. He spoke, and it came to be; He commanded, and it stood firm."[3] In other words, God created the cosmos without lifting a finger. And when He created the heavens, He did it all without the aid of a "how to make a universe" kit, an existing photo, a template, or a diagram. God was creating in the truest sense of the word, speaking the world into existence out of absolutely nothing.

God is the one who makes light fly.

He sits enthroned above the circle of the earth, and its people are like grasshoppers [to Him]. He stretches out the heavens like a canopy, and spreads them out like a tent to live in. "To whom will you compare me? Or who is my equal?" says the Holy One. Lift your eyes and look to the heavens: Who created all these? He who brings out the starry hosts one by one, and calls them each by name. Because of his great power and mighty strength, not one of them is missing.[4]

God is more massive than our wildest imagination, bigger than the biggest words we have to describe Him. And He's doing good today—sustaining galaxies, holding every star in place, stewarding the seemingly chaotic events of earth to His conclusion within His great story.

God is constant. He blinks and a lifetime comes and goes. To Him one day is like a thousand years and a thousand years like one day. All of human history could be written on His fingernail, with plenty of room left over for more.

And God is doing well today, thank you. He has no dilemmas. No quandaries. No counselors. No shortages. No rivals. No fears. No cracks. No worries. He is self-existent, self-contained, self-perpetuated, self-powered, and self-aware. In other words, He's God and He knows it.

HE IS TIMELESS. AGELESS.
CHANGELESS. ALWAYS.

After an eternity of being God, He shows no signs of wear and tear. He has no needs. His accounts are in the black. He's the owner, not to mention Creator, of all of the world's wealth and treasure. He made the gold and silver, and the trees we print our paper money on. He owns the cattle on a thousand hills, and all the hills the cows are standing on. He holds the patent on the skies above—not to mention the earth, the seas and their depths below, the breeze, the colors of the sunset and every flowering thing. They all are His invention. His design. His idea.

God does whatever He wants. His purposes are a sure thing. There's no stopping Him. No containing Him. No refuting Him. No cutting Him off at the pass. No short-circuiting His agenda. God is in control. He sends forth lightning from His storehouse, He breathes out the wind, waters the earth, raises up rulers, directs the course of nations, births life, ordains death, and, in the midst of it all, still has time to be intimately acquainted with the everyday affairs of everyone on the planet.

God knows everything about everything and everyone. His eyes race back and forth across the cosmos faster than we can scan the words on this page. There is not a bird flying through the air or perched on a branch that escapes His field of vision. He could start with Adam and name every man, woman, and child who has ever lived, describing every detail about each one. To Him, pitch darkness and midday are one and the same. Nothing is hidden from Him. He wrestles with no mysteries. He doesn't need to wait for a polygraph machine to decipher the truth. He sees clearly, and comprehends all He sees. He's never known what it is to have a teacher, a role model, an advisor, a therapist, a loan officer, an adjuster, a doctor, or a mother.

God's rule and reign are unrivaled in history and eternity. He sits on an everlasting throne. His Kingdom has no end. Little gods abound, but He alone made the heavens and the earth. God has never feared a power struggle or a hostile takeover. He doesn't have to watch His back. He has no equal. No peer. No competition.

It makes perfect sense that His name should be *I AM*.

And even more sense that my name is *I am not*.

You and I are tiny. Miniscule. Transient. Microscopic. A momentary and infinitesimal blip on the timeline of the universe. A seemingly undetectable alliance of dust particles held together by the breath of God.

The sum of our days is like a vapor—our accumulated efforts like chaff in the wind. Among us, even the richest of the rich owns nothing. The strongest of the strong can be felled in one faltering heartbeat. We are fleeting mortals. Frail flesh. Little specks. Phantoms.

If this fact makes you just a tad bit uncomfortable, you're not alone. Invariably, when I talk about the vastness of God and the cosmos, someone will say, "You're making me feel bad about myself and making me feel really, really small," as if that's the worst thing that could happen. But the point is not to make you *feel* small, rather to help you see and embrace the reality that you *are* small.

Really, really small.

But that's not where the story ends.

Though we are transient dust particles in a universe that is expanding faster than the speed of light, the unexplainable mystery of mysteries is that *you and I are loved and prized by the God of all Creation.*

Simply because He wanted to, He fashioned each of us in His own image, creating within us the capacity to know Him. And if that wasn't staggering enough, in spite of our foolishness and rebellious hearts, God has pursued us with relentless passion and patience, fully expressing to us His unfathomable love through the mercy and grace of the cross of His Son, Jesus Christ.

Sure, just a glimpse of His glory instantly resizes us to microscopic proportions. But God is not trying to deflate us with a Milky Way-sized put down that erodes any sense of self and reduces us to a pointless existence. Just the opposite. When we see just how tiny we are, our self-worth and our God-worth can become one and the same as we are stunned with the reality that we have been made in His very likeness and invited to know Him personally.

I am not, but He knows my name.

I am not, but He has pursued me in His love.

I am not, but I have been purchased and redeemed.

I am not, but I have been invited into The Story.

I am not, but I know the Creator of the universe.

I am not, but I know I AM!

Let the depth and wonder of the words sink in.

I am not, but I know I AM.

That's the complete story—the entire Gospel—the whole truth about who you are. You *are small,* but you can be on a first-name basis with *I AM.* You're beyond tiny, but every ounce of you has been bought and redeemed by God's Son. You are a galactic nobody—in fact 99.99999999999999999999999999999 percent of the people on earth have never heard of you. But God knows everything about you and calls you His own.

What more could we possibly achieve on earth that is

greater than what we already have? We are already friends of God. What greater prize or position could we hope to gain? What praise of men could eclipse the voice of *I AM* speaking to us by name?

One of the joys of knowing our new name—of celebrating that *I am not*—is that it allows you and me to bypass the all-too-familiar trap of thinking more highly of ourselves because of what we have accomplished or who we know. I'll never forget when that clicked for me.

I had just walked into a packed ballroom in Nashville during Gospel Music Association (GMA) week, where the who's who in Christian music gather for four days to network and honor the year's best with the Dove awards. The room was filled with artists, label heads, managers, booking agents, and just about anyone who was a somebody in the industry.

During the day, I kept noticing the elaborate name tags around everyone's neck. Marked with all kinds of special colored ribbons, the name tags were mini-billboards, broadcasting to those in attendance just how important, or unimportant, each of us was. You could see it everywhere, people crammed in elevators and huddled in conversations, straining to catch a glimpse of the critical data printed on everyone's badge. *Is he a somebody? Should I speak to her? Don't look now, but that's so and so!*

But I wasn't there to just hang around. I had been invited to speak at a luncheon sponsored by the WOW brand, a gathering attended by most all the power-people in the industry. My message for the day just so happened to be *I am not but I know I AM*. I felt nervous—not only because I was a peon representing a label most people had never heard of, but because I knew I was a visitor who'd been invited to bring encouraging words but who'd arrived carrying a stake that God was asking each of us to drive through the heart of self.

Well, somewhere during the message, after we had established the fact that all of our names are actually *I am not,* I suggested that the kind GMA folks could have saved a ton of money and streamlined the registration process by simply putting *I am not* on each name tag instead of our individual names. Not only would this simplify things (and spare us the embarrassment of forgetting the names of friends we hadn't seen in a while), it would be much more accurate and remind us all that the mission of our industry is clear—making much of Jesus until the whole world hears His name and sees His fame.

What a concept! And what a way to walk through life, entering every environment with every intention to shine as little light as possible on me and as much light as possible on the Son of God.

Later, I was happy to see a guy in the hallway with a

black mark through his name and the words *I am not* inscribed below. To complete the message the guy really needed to add the rest of the phrase, *but I know I AM!* That's the name tag!

We know God—and He knows us, too—inviting us to an intimate union made possible when He took an extraordinary step from the hugeness of heaven to the narrow streets of one small town on earth.

BEcame

The Church of the

Annunciation sits off a crowded, narrow street in the heart of Nazareth, the town where Jesus grew up. The church is so named because it was in this little village that the angel appeared to Mary announcing the miracle birth of God's Son.

Inscribed in the stone fascia high above the church's entrance are the words: *Verbo Caro Factum, est et Habitavit en Nobus.* Knowing little Latin, I leaned in to ask our guide for a translation.

"And the Word became flesh and dwelled among us," he said.

Of course, I thought.

Never did these words from the opening chapter of John's gospel seem more fitting. Closing my eyes, I could almost hear little boys running through the streets as they laughed their way through another summer afternoon. This is where Jesus played. Where He grew. This place was the neighborhood of the Savior of the world.

Just slightly up a hill at the end of a narrow, twisting alley is the site of the synagogue where, on that fateful Sabbath, Jesus shocked the world. Taking the scroll for the day's prescribed reading in His hands, He proclaimed, "The Spirit of the Lord is on me, because he has anointed me to preach good news to the poor. He has sent me to proclaim freedom for the prisoners and recovery of sight for the blind, to release the oppressed, to proclaim the year of the Lord's favor."

The clincher, however, was His closing line—"Today this scripture is fulfilled by the one reading it."[5] That's the claim that turned the religious world upside down. In fact, His claim to be fulfillment of Isaiah's prophecy was paramount to Him coming right out and saying He was the Son of God, an unbelievable proposition to those who knew so well that He was Mary's kid. In a heartbeat, pandemonium broke out and cries of "Blasphemy!" were on people's lips. The audience that moments before had been listening intently was now a mob chasing Jesus to the edge of town, trying to hurl Him off a cliff.

So much for being the hometown boy.

I quickly grabbed my journal and copied the inscription. Below the Latin words I wrote the verse in English and determined that for the next few days I would meditate on the words one at a time. Using what I call the "One-Word Bible Study," I would let the verse sink into my heart and mind by contemplating each successive word for an entire day. (See Appendix A, "The One-Word Bible Study Method".)

So the next morning I wrote the word "and" at the top of the page in my journal, and my "one word at a time" journey through John 1:14 began. What happened over the next few days astounded me, as words big and small opened the Story of God's redemptive heart right before my eyes.

My journey unfolded like this—

Yep. *And.* It all started with a simple conjunction. Three little characters. A throwaway word, right?

I know what you're thinking. There's no way I'm going to spend sixteen hours thinking about a conjunction. There's no possible way I'm going to spend an entire day meditating on the word *and*.

That's what I was thinking, too. But I determined to stick with *and*, even though I wanted to rush ahead to a more captivating and significant word.

And—the Word became flesh.

And.

Finally, after carrying around *and* in my heart for a good portion of the day, I saw it. Wow! Suddenly, *and* blew me away. In this verse *and* is not just a simple conjunction. No way. *And* is a huge statement—God's way of saying, "All the stuff in the Old Testament up to now has been pretty amazing, right? Well, fasten your seat belts, there's a whole lot more coming."

It was at this point that *and* started talking:

"Remember the power of God displayed at the Red Sea? That was amazing, but that's not all there is. Remember the visible glory of God that descended over the temple, causing everyone to hit the deck? That was awesome, but there's a greater glory coming. Remember Daniel, David, Joshua, Rahab, and the other men and women of faith? They all performed wonders, but the story doesn't stop with them. God is not finished. Stay tuned. The Son of God is on the way. Messiah is coming here and now. God has so much more in store."

And.

For me, day one was full-on. I went to sleep that night convinced that I had only seen the tip of the iceberg of God's activity in my life and in the world around me. Given that I had seen God do so much in my lifetime, it made my mind race at hyperspeed to think of all that was still to come.

Who says reading the Bible is a drag? I was inspired by the hope unlocked by a tiny article of speech called *and*.

Encouraged, I moved on.

Day 2: The.

Oh no, not again.

The, you're thinking. You spent a whole day meditating on the word *the*?

Pretty deep, huh? I had progressed from a conjunction to a definite article. From *and* to *the*. Not exactly the stuff of devotional ecstasy, right?

I'll admit, I had my doubts, too. But I went for it anyway. And it paid off. Big-time.

Turns out in this particular verse, the *the* is incredible, an integral component of what God is saying. You see, when God chose to do more (*and*), He didn't just do something, anything. God did a very specific thing, a you're-not-going-to-believe-what-I'm-about-to-do-now thing. God sent His Son, the living Word, into the streets of Nazareth in the form of a little boy.

Jesus wasn't one of many sons, He was *the* only Son. He wasn't one of a multitude of messengers sent from above, He was *the* message and messenger come down from heaven to earth.

God did one thing.

He sent one Son to be *the* way.

John doesn't write that *a* Word became flesh.

Or that *some* Word became flesh.

Or that *the flavor-of-the-day* Word became flesh.

Or that *a really good* Word became flesh.

And certainly not that *one of many* Words became flesh.

John carefully wrote *the* Word.

THE ONE WORD. THE DEFINITIVE WORD. THE ONE AND ONLY WORD— JESUS CHRIST.

On day two I fell in love with *the*, because *the* was all about the uniqueness of the Christ, the full and final revelation of God to man.

Day two was a really wonderful day.

Day 3. Word.

This day was all about the "big-W" Word, not the "small-w" one. The latter is all about the vocabulary of men, but the big, "capital W" Word is all about the language of God. Day three for me was a celebration of Jesus, the one who embodied everything God wanted to communicate to the whole wide world. Once again, after four hundred years of silence, God was talking, and Jesus was His one-Word proclamation.

Well, I think you're getting the hang of it by now, so I'll move on to—

<u>Day 4. Became.</u>

Honestly, I was still on overload from days one through three when I slowly penciled the word *became* in my journal. At first I thought *became* was going to fit more in the category of the words *the* and *and* in my one-word journey. But then God detonated *became* in my heart, obliterating the calm of a perfectly beautiful afternoon.

A breeze was blowing in from the Sea of Galilee toward the landscaped hillside—the place many claim to be the site where Jesus preached the Sermon on the Mount. Our group had scattered among the grounds of yet another sacred church to quietly reflect on His sermon's succinct words before heading back to the buses and moving on to another location.

I was sitting alone under a tree, staring at the word *became*, replaying the verse over and over in my mind. "And the Word *became* flesh, and dwelled among us."

Became.

I let that word settle into my heart. And I waited.

And then, right there in the quiet shade, the word *became* leaped off the page and shot through every fiber of my being. I wanted to scream, but couldn't for fear the nuns valiantly patrolling the grounds would expel me—not to mention I'd ruin a perfectly peaceful moment for everyone else in our group.

But I could barely control myself. There it was, right in

louieGIGLIO

front of me. *Became.* The gospel in one word—redemption's story shrunk down to six amazing letters.

Do you see it? *Became* is a compound word, meaning it is comprised of two words—the word *be* and the word *came*. Wow, now do you see it?

This verse is about Jesus, the one who bears the same name as the God who appeared to Moses at the burning bush. That day God revealed Himself to Moses as *I AM*—*I AM THAT I AM*—the present tense, active form of the verb, *to be.*

Or, simply, **BE.**

God told Moses His name is *BE,* the very name Jesus used when He claimed, "Before Abraham was, *I AM*" (John 8:58). Being God, Jesus' name is *I AM.* Jesus is *BE.* And *BE* is one of the two words in our compound word, *became.*

In an instant, *became* became *BE came,* and I wanted to shout for joy from that hillside.

Now the verse read, "And the Word—whose name is *BE*—came."

Wake the world. Jesus came! *BE* came! *I AM* came! But in a most surprising form. Right here for all to see, the Lord of Creation took on the dusty frame of a man. The great *I AM* became *I am not*—God spanning the gap to you and me in the person of His only Son. (See Appendix B, "Why the Beattitudes Are the BE Attitudes".)

BE came, because we could never get to *BE* on our own.

BE came so that we would know that we matter to God.

BE came to give us life again.

BE came to rescue us from the small and fleeting stories of us.

BE came to make a way for us to join the never-ending Story of God.

BE came, as a one-word summary of God's message of grace and mercy, the end of man's futile attempts at finding his way to Him, the deathblow to religious systems that attempt to lift us heavenward. God has come down to us—Jesus, walking on Planet Earth. Here.

Simply astounding.

And how did He come?

Day 5: Flesh.

BE came flesh. God arrived with skin, the Divine in the form of a sweaty, laughing boy playing with other kids in a narrow street on a summer afternoon.

That's how God chose to connect with us, to deliver us, to come for us.

He didn't send a note, an e-mail, a check, a cosmic event, a mandate, or an image on a toasted cheese sandwich. When God came to man—when *BE* came—*BE* became *flesh*. The God of the world in a body like yours and mine.

Why does it matter? Because you can touch flesh. You can identify with flesh. You can wrap your arms around flesh and feel its heartbeat. You can hear the voice of flesh and look into its eyes. And if you're searching for a sacrifice for the sins of all mankind, you can pierce flesh and it will bleed. You can nail flesh to a cross.

Day five was a reverent day—a celebration of divine incarnation, the staggering mystery of "the fullness of God in bodily form."

I have to admit I was so excited I began to race through the remaining words in the verse. *And the Word became flesh...and...dwelled...among...us.* Each one is revolutionary in its own way, crammed full of potential and meaning.

But jump ahead with me to the next sentence in the verse:

Day 10. And.

If it isn't enough that God wrapped Himself in human flesh and moved into the neighborhood, there's still more.

And...

Day 11. We.

All of us. You and me. Each of us. None excluded. The rich and poor of us. The good and bad of us. The high and low of us. The great and small of us. The old and young of us. Everyone of us. *We...*

Day 12: Beheld.

Hmm. I hope you're smiling by now, already ahead of me on this one.

We *BE* held. How miraculous is that? First, *BE* came. A mystery that is unfathomable in itself. But then, we *BE* held. We—you and me—put our arms out to touch and hold the Son of God. Embracing Him. Holding onto Him. Squeezing to our chests the very Creator of the world.

And notice how the *BE* in *Be-held* goes both ways. First we have "we *BE* held," meaning little tiny *I am nots* like you and me get to put our arms around the great *I AM*. But just as astonishing, we see that "*BE* held"—a beautiful picture of the God of the universe carefully wrapping His great arms of grace around you and me.

On that trip to Israel I saw them with my own eyes. Bethlehem. Nazareth. Calvary. Spots of earth that recount the story of Jesus becoming small. Real places that show us life is not about us trying to be bigger, but about embracing our smallness as we confess, *I am not...but I know I AM.* I've made it up that little road in Nazareth a few times now, and once I get my bearings, I can find the church on my own.

If only it were that easy to wake up and see the Story of God.

BIG river

It was a hot African morning when Shelley and I, and a small group of friends, finally made our way down what proved to be a treacherous, gorge-dropping descent to the Zambezi River below. If the trail that deposited us at the water's edge was any indication, we were already in over our heads—and we hadn't even gotten into the river. Upstream, we could hear the roar of Victoria Falls—at a mile wide, it is the world's largest waterfall, cascading over rugged cliffs where Zambia and Zimbabwe meet.

After a few last minute instructions from our guide Steve, we strapped on our helmets, wedged into our raft, and drifted out into the current.

Looking back on it now, I think we should have paid more attention to the dead hippopotamus we noticed swelling in the morning sun as it floated in a nearby eddy. The hippo, Steve explained, had probably gotten swept away by the river's strong currents and hurled over the falls to its death...

Initially the river was wide and inviting. We all had a good laugh at the first rapid when Steve purposely dumped us into the water. But as with the not-so-subtle message of the hippo, I should have considered Steve's words more carefully when he said, "You need to get used to being in the water. It's going to happen a lot today."

Getting wet wasn't such a big deal at first. In the water, out of the water—it all seemed like part of the adventure. Soon, though, the river narrowed, and the immense volume of water that flowed over the wide expanse of the falls began to squeeze into a narrow channel. As it cut its way between towering rocky cliffs, the mighty Zambezi created one class IV rapid after another, and a few monstrous class Vs. Fortunately, long stretches of quiet separated the rapids, but more and more, we spent the calm between the thundering white water dreading the inevitable.

As we drifted down toward each successive rapid, the roar of the approaching turbulence increased. Steve would shout out paddling orders, then, working as hard as we could, we'd do our best to aim the raft into the rapid at just the right angle. Our two objectives—to stay in the raft and to come out safely on the other side.

At rapid after rapid we failed, at least on the first objective. No matter how determined we were to stay above the river, the waves would catapult the raft as if it had been shot out of a cannon, sending bodies flying left and right into the raging waters.

By this time, all laughing had stopped and the panicking began—especially when we nearly lost a team member in the powerful current.

Thankfully, we found a way to walk around the last man-eating rapid (we were told this one was big enough to drag a bus under) before the midway point and were mercifully deposited alive and intact on a wide sandy bank. This hadn't been one of our better days. Exhilarating, yes. Enjoyable, not so much.

And now we were faced with a choice. We could hike up and out, or carry on. While we thought it over, Steve informed us the second leg of the journey was a lot more severe, with bigger rapids and crocodiles sunning on the banks along the way.

Right there, our group took a vote. It was unanimous. We'd had enough. The Zambezi was too much for us. The river had won.

Not so visible, but much more dangerous, is the current that still flows out of Eden. And guess what? We're all in it. More powerful than ten thousand Zambezis, the downstream effects of Adam's sin still sweep us into the danger zone, that place where sin deceives us and we live as though we are bigger than we truly are.

Call it River Pride, white water that provides a thrill while deluding us into believing we're in control. Just when we think we're riding the river, we find out the river is in control, hurling us overboard at will and sucking us under.

For proof we don't have to even look past earth's first human. Even though he had it all, the temptation to be as big as God was irresistible, and Adam stumbled and fell. When he sinned, he opened the floodgate of death and deception that robbed him, and us, of the joy that God intended.

It all started so well for Adam.

I mean, can you imagine waking up for the very first time to see the Creator of the universe staring back at you?

Adam must have been floored. (I wonder if the first words he heard were, "Welcome! Welcome to the Story of God.")

I don't know what was said that first morning, but I'm pretty sure Adam smiled back at God—once the gaping hole that was his mouth finally closed. After all, he was alone with God in a perfect world, having drawn his first breath from His, a living being uniquely wired for connectivity with the Divine. Then Eve arrived, made like Adam in the image of God, and all was well in Eden.

But soon the world's first couple realized that the story unfolding around them was not about them. Instead, they had arrived on day six of a seven-day Creation story. And the story was all about the creating One—a grand epic in which God alone played the leading role. (See Appendix C, "God's Passion for God's Glory.") Yes, the two of them were invited to rule over the beasts of the field and charged with populating the earth. But the whole world around them was already singing the Creator's praise before they ever made an appearance on earth's stage.

The mood in Paradise soured when Adam and Eve decided that their little supporting roles just weren't enough. They wanted a bigger stake. A higher profile. More of the limelight. They wanted to be as big as God.

Deceived, they believed the forbidden fruit was the ticket to the top, the one thing that would vault them to immortality.

But the fruit bit back, and Adam and Eve died, the first casualties of the pride that precedes every fall. Sadly, they didn't appreciate the fact that they were already immortal, carriers of the living breath of God. Sure they were small, but they were living out their days *in* the Story of God. Yes, they were the first to bear the names *I am not,* but they were also the first to know the wonder of intimately knowing *I AM.* Now, in a heartbeat, they were spiritually dead, abandoned to shrinking stories that would soon come to an end.

Do you see what I'm trying to show you here? When someone named *I am not* decides to live as though his or her name is really *I AM,* one consequence always follows: death.

WE GET SWEPT AWAY. SOONER OR LATER, WE, TOO, BECOME A CARCASS FLOATING IN THE SUN.

But let's not dwell on Adam and Eve. It doesn't take a magnifying glass to find the same temptation lurking within you and me. You'd think we'd learn from Eden's folly, but instead we seem more determined than ever to prove we're the exception to the rule, impervious to the current. We constantly thrust ourselves onto center stage, acting like life is ours to do with as we please—a drama that is all about me and mine.

We're not the only ones. It's been that way in every generation.

Even after the Flood, man continued to think of himself in glowing terms, grossly overestimating his position and power in the Story of God. After some time had passed, people said to one another:

> "Come, let's make bricks and bake them thoroughly.... Come, let us build ourselves a city, with a tower that reaches to the heavens, so that we may make a name for ourselves and not be scattered over the face of the whole earth."[6]

I'm not sure if they really believed God was only a few flights up, or if they were just sold on their ability to build a tower to eternity. One thing I do know—they were squarely in the current of the Fall, once again seeking to make a name for themselves when all the while they already had one. But, I guess building a memorial to the name *I am not* was not nearly glamorous enough.

Apparently, that's still the case today, wouldn't you say?

Things go terribly wrong when we try to assume control of our lives and those around us. For one, we sentence ourselves to a heavy load—we call it the weight of the world—

that God never intended for us to carry. Running our world is too much for us, no matter how hard we try. To try to be God—something I find I am really bad at—without having the wisdom and power of God is a ridiculous proposition, a daunting task. Attempting to orchestrate the world around us, even for a day, leaves us stressed and spent.

But there's an even greater downside to spending our lives making ourselves out to be bigger than we are. The danger is that we might succeed—at least in earthly terms—in making a name for ourselves. We might draw a crowd, grab some fame, amass some riches, hear the roar of applause. We might succeed at building a tower to the sky with our name emblazoned on it. All that hard work, only to have the River Pride deposit us on a sandbar called "The End." And in that moment, when the tiny story of us comes to a close, all the glory we could garner for ourselves will fade to nothing.

Fortunately, there's another way to spend our lives.

If you've ever been in really big currents, you know it's pointless to try to swim against them. It's no different with the River Pride coming out of Eden. It's the most destructive current of all. Left to ourselves we could never swim to safety. Even with our greatest effort, we cannot escape its power.

The good news is we don't have to. We're invited to accept, as a free gift, rescue from sin's deadly flow and a place in God's eternal glory, a place we don't deserve, but one He offers us to share in through the death of His Son. The one requirement is that we trade the starring role in the miserably small stories of us for supporting roles in the great Story of God.

How?

Jesus became—*BE came*—small so that we could reach our highest and fullest potential in Him. He came down to lift us up out of microscopic stories that only get swallowed up in the grave and place us in the river of His life that leads us home. He gave Himself for us so that we could die to self-fame, self-glory, self-effort, self-centeredness, and the self-stories that are quickly coming to an end.

I like to call it *glorious death*—our giving up our lives for something far greater.

That's exactly what Jesus did, and what we, too, are called to do with our lives.

> Your attitude should be the same as that of Christ Jesus: Who, being in very nature God, did not consider equality with God something to be

grasped, but made himself nothing, taking the very nature of a servant, being made in human likeness. And being found in appearance as a man, he humbled himself and became obedient to death—even death on a cross! Therefore God exalted him to the highest place and gave him the name that is above every name, that at the name of Jesus every knee should bow, in heaven and on earth and under the earth, and every tongue confess that Jesus Christ is Lord, to the glory of God the Father.[7]

Jesus' death is the epitome of "glorious death"—death that leads to glorious and never-ending life.

In the same way, when we come to the end of ourselves, we're suddenly ready for God to do in and through us what we could never do on our own. His life and power bring the possibility of the supernatural activity of God to little *I am nots* like you and me. Not only do we know *I AM,* but *I AM* lives in us. He displays His power in us and glorifies His name through us. And in so doing we stake our claim in immortality, sowing our lives for His renown, investing in the applause of heaven that never, ever ends.

I'm not sure I'm going down the Zambezi again, even if I have the chance. But I'm positive today that I don't have to be swept away by the current of deception. What about you? Are you feeling the exhilaration of being on top of the wave?

Or are you feeling the undertow dragging you down?

The truth is we can be free of sin's power when we die to pride and self, and live instead in the powerful current of Christ's life in us—that eternal kind of life flowing in the veins of all who put their trust in Him.

the little LEADER

Nobody likes

coming in second, or third—or worse. No, something in us wants to always be on top, and somewhere deep within we quietly rejoice when our competition hits a snag or collapses.

Nowhere is this human tendency more apparent than when we're called to lead. Leaders must take a special responsibility for defining and reaching success (usually that means coming in first). You might find yourself in the leadership spot on a team or in a small group, in business, sports, music, education, or ministry. But wherever you are in a leadership role, prepare to get hit hard and fast by the impulse to be the biggest and finish first.

I imagine John's coworkers were in hyperventilation mode as they arrived with the news that his operation—and theirs—was no longer the biggest shop around. It appears the disciples of Jesus had taken up baptizing—in the same river, no less—and were drawing crowds that dwarfed those that were still coming to John.

You see, John was the first guy in the baptism business. Thus the name we still know him by today—John the Baptist. Technically, he was the *first* Baptist. Like me, some of you may have grown up going to the First Baptist Church in your town, but let's face it, John had the real thing—the very first Baptist church. A forerunner to Jesus Christ, John preached the good news of the coming Messiah, urging people to repent and prepare the way for the Lord. Soon crowds were flocking to hear him teach and people were being baptized in the waters of the Jordan River. In time, his reputation reached the Jewish religious leaders in Jerusalem and, curious, they dispatched some priests to investigate.

The political and religious climate in those days was tense. Four hundred years had passed since any visible sign of God's activity—four centuries of silence without any prophet, any voice. The entire Jewish world was on edge, suppressed by the Roman Empire, but on the lookout for anything that might signal the arrival of the Messiah, the Promised One of God. Now John was pulling in huge revival crowds out by the Jordan River, and the Jewish leaders went to check things out.

Being in ministry most of my life, I can imagine how I might have felt if my operation had grown so much that it caught the attention of the "big dogs" at headquarters and they had come down to see firsthand what was going on. Arriving on the crowded scene, the priests approached John and asked, "Who are you?"

> If there was ever a moment to stand in the spotlight, this was it.

If there was ever an opportunity for John to take credit, snag some glory, and grab the headlines, the moment had come. There he was, a simple prophet, surrounded by devoted followers and some of the top religious leaders of the day. "How'd you build such a big ministry?" they began. "What's the key to your baptizing success? What do you have to say for yourself?"

But John knew exactly what (actually Who) they were looking for. And he knew what he had come to do. So when asked about his identity, when given the chance to take center stage, John "did not fail to confess, but confessed freely, 'I am not the Christ.'"[8]

Notice the double use of the same phrase in his answer. John did not fail to confess, but confessed freely, "I am not the Christ." In other words, when it came time to either be the star of the show or shine the light on someone else, John immediately directed the attention to the one he was called to serve.

And did you catch his opening five words? *I am not* the Christ.

Amazing! John seemed to know his name was *I am not.* (Some of you thought I was making this whole "my name is *I am not"* thing up.)

They asked again, "Then who are you? Are you Elijah?"

John said, "I am not."

They persisted. "Are you the Prophet?"

He answered, "No."

Finally they said, "Who are you? Give us an answer to take back to those who sent us. What do you have to say about yourself?"

Taking a deep breath (and having already clearly stated his *I am not* identity), John replied in the words of Isaiah the prophet:

"I am the voice of one calling in the desert, 'Make straight the way for the Lord.'"

Now some Pharisees who had been sent questioned him, "Why then do you baptize if you are not the Christ, nor Elijah, nor the Prophet?"

"I baptize with water," John replied, "but among you stands one you do not know. He is the one who comes after me, the thongs of whose sandals *I am not* worthy to untie."[9]

It's as if John was saying:

"Oh, I know you're looking for the Savior of Israel, but that's not me, even though it looks like we have a pretty major enterprise going on here and a ton of followers. I wouldn't dare take one iota of His attention or glory in this moment because I know who He is and who I am not. You're looking for the Christ, but I am not He. I am just one little voice in the drama, one small mouthpiece crying out in the midst of a barren land, saying, 'Get ready, Messiah is coming.'

I'm just a man. Yet, the One whose coming I announce is Holy God. He's everything. And though I prepare the way for His arrival and baptize in His name, I'm not worthy to even hold His shoes at the door. Please, don't mistake me for Him. My name is *I am not.* You're looking for **I AM.**"

The next day John was again baptizing in the Jordan when he saw Jesus coming toward him. I imagine his heart was now firmly lodged in his throat, but John managed to shout for all to hear, "Behold,[10] the Lamb of God who takes away the sin of the world!"[11]

John knew who Jesus was, and when the moment arrived he turned, pointed his finger, and exclaimed, "There He is,"—or as we have in some translations, "Behold."

I know *behold* is an outdated word in our culture (if you don't believe me, just try to work it into a conversation or two today). But think about it with me. In the spirit of our One-Word Bible Study method, *behold* can be understood as a one-word summary of what Christ's appearing was all about.

BE hold. I AM hold.

Jesus' very presence on the banks of the Jordan that day was God's proclamation that He wanted to wrap His Holy arms around us all—an invitation for us to reach out and take hold of Him. Like in the case of "we *BE* held," "behold" suggests the mysterious possibility that each of us can find our place in the eternal embrace of the God of the whole wide world.

And how was it going to happen? Because the Lamb of God was now stepping into redemption's story, taking on the sin of every human who would ever live. *BE* was going to be able to hold us—and invite us to cling to Him—through the sacrifice of Jesus Christ and the gift of grace He would afford to all men.

"Behold!" John cried. "There's the One we've all been waiting for!" Every head turned to look at Jesus Christ, the eyes of an entire crowd now riveted on one man. But scan the crowd and see if you can find John. Just a sentence ago all eyes were on him. All the attention was his. People hung on his every word. Now he was out of the spotlight, just another face in the crowd with his eyes glued on Jesus.

And John seems so content—and even genuinely thrilled—to point people away from himself to one he believed was greater. As the crowd locked its gaze on the Christ, he continued, "This is the one I meant when I said, 'A man who comes after me has surpassed me because he was before me.'"[12]

I don't know about you, but that verse makes my head spin. John knew that even though Jesus came after him chronologically, He was already in the story before him. Jesus may have just arrived in Galilee, but His name was *I*

AM, meaning He had existed forever. From this, John deduced correctly that since Jesus existed long before he ever baptized the first person, Jesus was far greater than he could ever hope to be. John never thought his ministry outfit was number one because the very one his ministry was about had already far surpassed anything he would ever do.

Like John, all *little leaders* know who comes first in the story. When they do accomplish great things or taste success, they do so with the realization that God had been on the scene for a long, long time, and that He is the source of their vision, gifting, opportunity, creativity, energy, and breath. (No matter where we finish among men, Christ already has a permanent hold on first place.)

That's why John was never happier than the day all eyes turned to Jesus.

If you don't believe it, notice what happened the next day. John was talking to two of his disciples (for "his disciples," you could insert "his team," "his key staff," "his church members," or, "the guys he had poured his life into") when he saw Jesus walking by. The implication from the Gospel account is that John's guys didn't see Jesus right away, and might not see him at all.

So what's going to happen? Sure, yesterday Jesus had

His moment to shine, but you have to wonder what might have been going through John's mind now.

Was it, "Oh no, not Him again"? Or, "Hey, He got His props yesterday; let's get the focus back on me today"?

Nope. Once again, John announced for all to hear, "Behold, the Lamb of God!" John wanted *everyone* to see Him. That's why he shouted, "There He goes again!" John went way beyond the calculated and polite response of giving Jesus the platform for a day—you know, that kind of false humility that somehow seems to telegraph its true intent no matter what we say. Instead, he showed his true colors as again and again he deflected the focus from himself to God. In fact, something in his voice (and eyes) was so sincere and convincing that two of his disciples turned and left him to follow Jesus. Imagine that. Two guys you have invested in and led well, now turning away from you to follow someone else.

But that's what John was all about.

John was a little leader.

I don't mean he was small in stature or vision or courage, or short on influence. Just that John knew who he wasn't—

AND WHO HE IS.

There's something pretty powerful about knowing who

you are—and knowing who you're not. Because John knew his name was *I am not*, he was free from—

—the seduction of fame,

—the tyranny of comparison,

—the delusional current of self-deception,

—the never-ending scramble to the top of the heap,

—ego,

—jealousy,

—backbiting,

—a massively swollen head.

And he was free from the ultimate rip-off—holding onto the starring role in a tiny story that was quickly vanishing from view.

No matter who you are, it's hard to stay on top forever, and it wasn't long until the new baptizer in town knocked John's operation from the top of the perch. At least that's what John's followers were spewing when they reported "Rabbi, that man who was with you on the other side of the Jordan—the one you testified about—well, he is baptizing, and everyone is going to him."[13] Who was the new kid on the baptizing block? He was none other than Jesus Himself, and—surprise, surprise—everyone was going to Him.

There's nothing that gets under our skin or tests our

motives more than the size of someone else's crowd, and John's team was raging with envy. After all, this Jesus fellow had come to them to be baptized in the first place, and for all they knew He looked around, stole their ideas and methods, and then had the nerve to go right down the street and open up a baptizing operation of His own. Oh sure, even though *His* ministry was bigger, they could still stake their claim as "first." But for now they wanted John to fight back and take some kind of action against this idea-stealing newcomer.

But John knew his name was *I am not.*

In fact, he said it again for good measure. "A man can receive only what is given him from heaven. You yourselves can testify that I said, '*I am not* the Christ, but am sent ahead of him.'"[14]

He continued, "The bride belongs to the bridegroom. The friend who attends the bridegroom waits and listens for him, and is full of joy when he hears the bridegroom's voice. That joy is mine, and it is now complete." John was happy. His mission was accomplished. His role in the story faithfully executed. The Groom had arrived and he was the best man. *I am not but I know I AM.*

And then John uttered the words that pierce the flesh but free the soul: "He must become greater; I must become less."[15]

Let that phrase sink deep into your being:

HE MUST BECOME GREATER,
and I must become less.

John didn't politely say, "He should increase." Or, "I want Him to increase." Or even, "It would be nice if He did increase." John's confession was not about tipping his hat to the Son of God. Rather it was an expression of focused determination, a calculated purpose statement for life and ministry. It's as if John was saying:

> "No matter what else happens there's one thing that has to take place—one thing that must happen—and the one thing that must happen is that Jesus must emerge and expand in the hearts and affections of people. He must be elevated, honored, exalted, focused on, cherished, enjoyed, amplified, and adored by all people everywhere."

John's mission was simple and clear: Jesus must increase, and I must decrease. Convinced and aware that Jesus was center stage in the story, John found great joy and compelling purpose in pointing others to Him. His is the voice of the "little leader," a man so blown away by the privilege of knowing God personally that he couldn't be distracted by petty clashes and glory wars.

Jesus was on a meteoric rise. In the short time since His baptism by John in the Jordan, Jesus had called disciples and established a core team, performed the first recorded miracle at a wedding up the road in Cana, and spoken to Nicodemus in the night about being born again, uttering the words of John 3:16—words that have become the most well-known in Scripture. Jesus was clearly in a league of His own. But sadly, John's followers had been so busy trying to protect their turf they failed to notice that the kingdom had landed in the neighborhood. That kind of myopic, "it's all about me" vision, is the crippling byproduct of not knowing who He is and who we are not, a truth John embraced and championed.

"The one who comes from above is above all," the Gospel records. "The one who is from the earth belongs to the earth, and speaks as one from the earth. The one who comes from heaven is above all."[16]

In John's mind he wasn't losing his people to a bigger ministry. He was just doing what he came to do—holding wide the door for the arrival of heaven's King.

BE still

Even God rests.

That must have come as a huge shock to earth's first couple on the morning of Day Seven, their first full day on the job. After all, they had just arrived in God's Creation Story and were now in charge of managing the Garden God had made. Adam and Eve were together in love, a perfect match in a perfect world. They had no past, no baggage, no regrets, and no stress. Life was good.

That's why it's not hard to imagine their excitement when they awakened to their first full day on the planet. No doubt opening their eyes to the brilliant colors of the sunrise overloaded their senses and got their adrenaline pumping. The breeze, cool on their skin, carried a thousand glorious scents. The chorus of birds sounded like Beethoven to virgin ears. The man and woman were fully alive, armed with a vital mission and eager to get to work.

But just as they were hammering out their to-do list for the day, the voice of God rang out through Eden. "Good morning guys, it's me, the Lord! Welcome to Day Seven. Everybody doing okay? I hope you had a great night's sleep and you're feeling good. Today is going to be a special day, an amazing day. It's your very first day here with Me, and you're going to love it."

So far so good, they were thinking. But then God's morning wake-up call took an unexpected turn. "I'm not going to work today," He continued, "and I don't want you to either. Creation is complete. The universe is finished. Every star and each grain of sand is in place. The job is done. So let's just pause and drink it all in. Let's stop and consider what I have accomplished. Today, we celebrate all that I have made. That means no work today, my friends. Today is a day of rest!"

"A day of rest?" I can hear Adam protesting. "But, Lord, we're not the slightest bit tired! We just got here and we're ready to get busy doing what You have asked us to do. Why do we need to spend the whole day resting?"

I'm not sure if that's actually what Adam said, but I have a strong suspicion the questions raced through his mind. Here was a guy with a brand new job to do, and the thing that made the least sense to him on Day Seven was rest. He and Eve hadn't even been alive for twenty-four hours. I mean, don't you at least have to *live* a full day before you can take a day off?

Adam and Eve were feeling fine. They weren't stressed-out, overwhelmed, road-weary, overworked, vacation-starved, frazzled, worn down, bleary-eyed, overcommitted, or spent. Why would they possibly need a rest day this early in the game?

But maybe it was God who needed a break. After all, He was the one who had done all the creative work. Maybe He was the one who needed a rest. Right?

Wrong.

God wasn't the slightest bit tired on Day Seven. The Genesis account makes no reference to God sleeping or taking a break, or needing to. Making a world wasn't too much for Him. In fact, Genesis tells us God simply spoke and the world came into being. In other words, He made the universe without so much as lifting a finger. It wasn't as if God had collapsed after six days of labor and needed just a few more winks before getting started on a new day's work. No, God felt the same on Day Seven as He had before He invented time and space. On Day Seven, He was just as omnipotent (a big theological word that means God possesses an unlimited supply of energy) as He had always been.

So, if it wasn't exhaustion that caused God to take a break on Day Seven, what does it mean that He "rested" from all His work? I think it simply means God paused.

And why did He pause? Because He's God and He works at whatever pace He desires. God has never had a boss, a supervisor, a deadline, an assignment, or a project due date. He does what He wants, when He wants. And after six days of creative genius, God stopped to celebrate all that He had done. He stepped back and took time to admire His efforts, and to receive glory from all of Creation.

So let's recap: On Eden's first Sunday we find a man and a woman in perfect condition who have never known what it means to be tired, and we have a God who has known nothing but superabundant energy forever. Together, the three of them are ceasing from all labor to celebrate earth's inaugural day by…resting. Interesting.

Sabbath is funny like that.

You see, Sabbath is not so much about a day off as it is a "day up"—a day to remember that He is God and we are not. Without Sabbath, we forget who we are and lose sight of who He is, leaving us to carry the weight of the world on our shoulders. When there is no Sabbath in our lives we become intoxicated by the lie that the sum of our lives depends on our effort alone. We get to the place where we truly believe that the outcome of the story fully depends on us.

But in truth, we are tiny, limited beings. Our biggest and best efforts still accomplish far less than what God can do in us, through us—or without us—in one breath.

Enter Moses. Again.

Time has passed. Pharaoh has been defeated. Israel has been liberated by God's sovereign power. And once again, Moses is descending the same Mt. Sinai where he had encountered the burning bush and heard his divine invitation.[17]

Talk about a mountaintop experience. Moses had been up there alone on God's turf again. Mercifully God had covered Moses by His hand in a crag in the rock while the back of God's glory passed by. Moses couldn't see God's face and live, but trust me he wasn't disappointed. He had nearly died from the brightness of the backside of God's glory. Coming down that mountainside, his face literally glowed. I think he was terrified—and thrilled to still be breathing.

This time, Moses carries down with him two stones inscribed by the very finger of I AM. Of the ten simple rules for godly living written there, one is a Sabbath command. It reads:

> Remember the Sabbath day, to keep it holy. Six days you shall labor, and do all your work, but the seventh day is a Sabbath to the LORD your God. On it you shall not do any work, you, or your son, or your daughter, your male servant, or your female servant, or your livestock, or the sojourner who is within your gates. For in six days the LORD made heaven and earth, the sea, and all that is in them, and rested the seventh day. Therefore the LORD blessed the Sabbath day and made it holy.[18]

Obviously, all of the commands are crucial (after all, there were only ten of them) but this one stands out because of the sheer volume of the words it contains. It's easily the longest of them all, comprised of ninety-seven words. Compare that to the last six commandments, which together total only seventy-six words, and you get the feeling God is trying to make a point. Apparently, Sabbath rest is not just a suggestion for the betterment of your life and mine, but an essential, nonnegotiable command, an intrinsic part of the rhythm of life.

Clearly, Sabbath is about ceasing from labor, but at its core Sabbath is about a whole lot more than sleeping in or catching a nap. Sabbath rest is about a state of mind, a deep-seated belief that God is the creator and sustainer of all things—an acknowledgement that He is sufficient and that He can be trusted. Because one of the symptoms of sin is short-term memory loss, we quickly forget that He set in motion the entire universe before we arrived on the scene. We need to get our memories corrected and our trust renewed by stopping long enough to remember that His name is *I AM* and our names are *I am not*.

The instructions Moses delivered require us to "remember the Sabbath day, to keep it holy." But what does it mean to keep the Sabbath holy? Well, the word *holy* conveys moral purity—and God is the very definition of pure—but the word also implies "set apart." When we say God is holy, we are saying that He is not like any other thing. God is "other" (you could say He is completely unique—*uniquely* unique). He is unsurpassed in beauty and worth, forever and always the greatest thing in existence. There is no one like Him—never has been and never will be.

IN OTHER WORDS, GOD IS HOLY.

If that's holy, and the Sabbath is supposed to be a holy day, then the Sabbath could be called, "There's No One Like Our God Day."

Or...

"God Is Not Like Anybody Else Day!"

"I Am the Lord Day."

"Make No Mistake About It—I Can Do Anything Day."

"Wow! Look What God Has Done Day!"

Or simply...

"*I AM* Day."

To remember the Sabbath and to keep it holy is for us to say:

Everything doesn't hinge on me.

If I stop doing my part, the whole world will not fall apart.

I am not in control.

God made the world in six days without any input from me, or my assistance.

God doesn't need me to accomplish His work.

I am little.

God is huge.

I trust Him.

I think that's what the psalmist had in mind when he wrote, "God is our refuge and strength, an ever present help in trouble." And, "The LORD Almighty is with us; the God of Jacob is our fortress."[19] But notice how the first-

louie GIGLIO

person voice of God emerges at the end of this song with a Sabbath call. "Be still, and know that I am God; I will be exalted among the nations, I will be exalted in the earth."[20]

Let's face it, stillness is not exactly easy to come by in today's culture. We are far more likely to be restless, anxious, fearful, worrisome, and busy. But God's invitation is to be still—and to find again, in the calm pause, the assurance that He is, in fact, God. His plans are undeterred, and with or without us, He is going to receive glory from all peoples on the face of the earth.

But how do we find stillness when finances are tight, tragedy overwhelms, the kids seem out of control, nations are at war, relationships are strained, and there's just too much left to do at the end of the day?

It's simple. *Still* is found right next to *Be.*

See it?

"BE STILL, AND KNOW THAT I AM GOD."

That's right, the only place true stillness of the soul can be found on Planet Earth is in super-close proximity to the God of all Creation. Sabbath rest is in His lap. Our inner calm waits within His embrace. Our peace of mind is found in the assurance that God is present wherever we are.

Like with Adam and Eve, we begin our mission on earth by doing nothing. Yep, *nothing*. We begin everyday believing that God is already at work accomplishing His agenda, fulfilling His plans. We live each day like it was the very first day, a day that began at night, the time of day when we sleep and God works.

It's right there in the very first words of the Bible:

In the beginning God created the heavens and the earth. Now the earth was formless and empty, darkness was over the surface of the deep, and the Spirit of God was hovering over the waters.[21]

Day One began in absolute darkness, a place where no one could have worked even if they wanted to.

And God said, "Let there be light," and there was light. God saw that the light was good, and he separated the light from the darkness. God called the light "day," and the darkness "night." And there was evening and morning—the first day.[22]

I'll have to admit I didn't catch the day/night sequence on my own. I needed a little help from my friend John

David Walt to notice that a day doesn't begin in the morning, but at night. "And it was evening and morning, the first day." In other words, night comes first, where darkness reigns, morning in the middle, and then daytime, which fades into night where a new day begins again. That seems a little odd to us, and maybe even backward, but it makes perfect sense in the economy of God. John David says it like this: "We go to sleep and God goes to work. And we wake up to see what God has done."

Oh, we still go to work when we wake up, but as we go we carry the spirit of Sabbath rest with us, believing that we have been invited into an already-in-progress Story in which God was doing just fine long before our little feet ever hit the floor.

It's a little like what happens when our favorite TV show is interrupted by a late-breaking, "this just in" news story. After being transported halfway around the globe for some major development, or across town for a sensational car chase, we are sent on our way with the announcement, "Now we join the regularly scheduled program already in progress." In an instant, we are whisked back to our show, but sadly we have missed some of the action and have to spend the next few minutes trying to figure out what happened while we were away.

In a way, that's the story of our lives. Everywhere we go we walk into a story in motion. Before we ever arrive, God is on the scene carrying out His plan and causing all things to work for His fame. We arrive to join the regularly scheduled program already in progress.

So often we think that everything begins when we step through the door. We think the project happened because we had the brilliant idea, and are convinced that the mission was accomplished because we chose to participate. But things don't start when *we* have a "vision," or *we* think of a new way of doing things, choose to act, have a burst of creative inspiration, give, or pray. God's Story is the already-in-motion story, a story that was happening just fine before we arrived and is going to go on just fine with or without you and me.

That's why we should wake up each day on the lookout for the Story of God, constantly thinking to ourselves, "God is already here. *What is He up to?*"

I don't know about you, but I have to admit that Sabbath has not been a strong suit for me. I think that's partly because I was raised in a church culture and now live in a ministry world that has made Sunday a busy day. And it's partly because I have an inner drive that tends to push me past my limits. And it's partly—no, *all*—because I have a corrupted flesh steeped in sin that is determined to prove to the world that I can live life and accomplish great things on my own.

But the truth is, I can't do anything on my own. Every

ounce of energy and each breath is a gift from God. And the life He requires of me—a life of goodness and godliness—is impossible for me to fully attain. I can't even keep those ten simple rules He gave Moses on the mountaintop.

Can you?

Fortunately, one of the great and mysterious joys of the Christian life is the reality of Christ's life within—a source of power and a quality of life that allows me to be all God calls me to be. That's why Paul writes of a new mystery when he exclaims, "[It] is Christ in you, the hope of glory."[23] He does not say it's Christ *and* you that brings the hope of a glorious life, but Christ *in* you. In other words, Sabbath is not about God and me operating as a dynamic duo. Sabbath rest is about me realizing that He is the only one capable of doing anything eternal in and through me.

That's the complete story of the gospel—not just a better destination when we die, but a new power source within for every day that we live. To tap into that power source—the endless spring of Christ's life—is to experience Sabbath on a whole new level. That's the story of amazing grace, the hope of anybody in touch with just how small they are, and a truth I was reminded of one afternoon during a walk on an Alabama beach.

FURIOUS rest

I like to accomplish
things. I like to dream, and often I see things that don't exist and try to figure out how to make them come to life. I like to build things and I'm into innovation and progress. I don't mind work. I respect productivity. But there's a downside. If I'm not careful, on the way to attempting something great for His name I can forget that mine is *I am not.*

That's where I was a few summers ago as I paced the shore on a south Alabama beach. I was so caught up in my thoughts I barely noticed the steady rhythm of the waves that were washing across my feet. In less than twenty-four hours the meeting to end all meetings (or at least, so I thought) was going down. For me—and the ministry of Passion Conferences—it was a pretty massive deal. On the table was the kind of opportunity that doesn't come along too often, and one that I never thought would be possible for us.

Two leaders from one of Christian music's most successful companies were on their way to meet with me at a beachside location where my family was on vacation. Yep, that's right—the big guys coming to me (insert first clue that I wasn't thinking straight). Within hours we would be across from one another and I already knew what was going to be on the table. I would have one shot (just one chance, so I thought) to make our case. For me, it felt like a do-or-die moment.

So there I was, storming up and down the beach, rehearsing my presentation over and over, less than six feet from an ocean more vast than my wildest imagination. But I hardly noticed. Instead, I felt like a thousand-pound weight was strapped to my chest.

I frantically tried to tally everything associated with my life and ministry that could be considered strength. First there were all the places I had spoken and the crowds I had stood in front of. Then there were the Passion gatherings and the records sold. We had a solid track record, not to mention future potential and the collected gifts and abilities of those on our team. Our upside seemed huge—and I was determined to squeeze every last ounce of persuasion out of it I could.

To put it straight, I was trying to impress these guys with our cause, hoping to convince them a venture with our team was something they should pursue.

I wish I could tell you that I was at rest—that I was acting on the fact that everything was in the hands of God. Obviously, I wasn't. I had been seduced into thinking that what happened the next day was pretty much all up to me.

Suddenly I sensed God's voice. "Why are you so perplexed by all of this?" He asked. "Why are you trying to make yourself seem so big and important? Louie, what you need to do before this meeting is to remember that you are

really, really small."

Whoa..., I thought. *Me? Small? Oh, yeah, that's right! Okay, I'll be small. What a brilliant approach. What an amazing strategy! Tomorrow, when they show up, I'll go in with a super-low profile. I'll go in acting all small, and just when their defenses are down, wham!—I'll jump up and surprise them with our strength!*

What a great plan. "Thank You, Lord," I replied. "This is an incredible idea."

This time His voice seemed a little more firm. "No, Louie, you're not following Me here. I'm not saying you should go into the meeting acting small. I'm telling you that you *are* small."

Oh.

As those words bounced around in my heart, the truth finally started sinking in. I *am* small.

Very small.

After only a few more steps my anxiety started to lift. Who was I kidding anyway? As much as I may have wanted to believe otherwise, I was neither big nor important. And Passion, the ministry we had poured our lives into for years, was nothing more than a tiny cog in God's kingdom venture, which is an immeasurable enterprise that spans the globe and bridges generations. By comparison, Passion was small-time, and I was even smaller—just a little guy who has been chosen by God to play an incredibly small role in one little chapter of His expansive story.

In a heartbeat, my game plan for the meeting changed. As I embraced the reality of my true size, a point that now seemed to be underscored by the countless grains of sand between my toes, the peace of God came rushing over me. Instantly, the weight was gone and I could breathe again. Instead of suffocating under the weight of thinking I was in control, I could now rest in the fact that God could do whatever He wanted with me—and I believed that He was going to do just that.

I didn't decide to skip out on the meeting, or pass on the chance to make our case. I just settled into my new size, and committed right there to open the meeting by confessing the truth about how small I really was.

Before long, I was sitting face-to-face with these two powerful music guys in a hotel suite. I was still a little nervous (okay, maybe a lot nervous), but it was the nervous that naturally comes with being in situations we've never been in before, not the other kind that feels like heart-crushing pressure because we think the fate of the world is in our hands. It's a better kind of nervous.

After the usual pleasantries and small talk, I said to them, "Before we begin, I just need to say something. When you get right down to it, I am very small, and our team is very small. We'd love to give this partnership a shot, but we are small-time players in God's kingdom story."

A pretty persuasive opening line, huh? But with those words came rest. And the assurance that God is huge and completely capable of accomplishing His purposes for our lives.

Let's be honest, trying to be God is pretty heady stuff for humans.

That's why each new week is to begin with a day called Sabbath. And every day is to be filled with the attitude of Sabbath rest. But, remember, the current of self is deceptively strong. So strong, in fact, that Sunday is slowly being blurred into Monday, and nobody in the church or the world seems to care.

Well, nobody except the folks with the humorous cow commercials.

Growing up in Atlanta I have always been partial to Chick-fil-A, a fast-food restaurant chain based here that enlists cows to help sell humans on eating chicken. Granted, I'm biased because my dad sketched the original Chick-fil-A logo back in 1964 and it's still in use today, but I'm also a fan of their unrivaled chicken sandwich, addictive sweet tea, and homemade lemonade. But what I love most about Chick-fil-A is that they are closed on Sundays. Yep, lights out, bars down in the food court at the mall.

It's interesting that these guys don't seem to be losing any money. On the contrary, the company is expanding rapidly. But even if they were losing ground to their competition by being closed one day a week, would that be a bad thing? I think the folks at Chick-fil-A are doing exactly what God had in mind way back in the Garden. They've created a great product (something it seems obvious to me that God-followers should do), forged a memorable (and apparently effective) ad campaign, and worked really, really hard—creating great demand for their product and a loyal following. They have faithfully served the American consumer Monday thru Saturday for almost sixty years. And on Sundays they've closed the doors and gone to worship, and in the process honored God not with busyness, but with stillness. Their unattended drive-through lines proclaim that they really do believe in the God who formed the universe without their help, or anyone else's.

Some of us forget, though. On more than one occasion, Shelley and I have been out on a Sunday afternoon, and craving some Chick-fil-A sweet tea, pulled expectantly into a drive-through only to wait at the order point for someone to talk to us from the little speaker box. There was even the time we honked impatiently. It took a while for us to look up and notice that we sat in a one-car line and there were no other cars in the parking lot.

But some of us forget more than just what day it is. We forget the simple truth of Sabbath rest, believing that the only way to stay on top is to work 365 days a year. Or worse, we take Sunday off, but make sure the people who work for us keep our operation running seven days a week. We're afraid that if we stop working we'll lose ground to the competition, give up market share, miss the deal, or fall behind the pack.

But I take you back to a chicken sandwich and sweet tea. These guys at Chick-fil-A have gained so much respect with consumers that mall managers will allow them to break ranks with other stores and shut their doors on the first day of the week.

How could you and I "remember the Sabbath, to keep it holy"? Taking rest seriously doesn't mean laziness or lack of momentum. It's not a "Let's just sit back in the easy chair of life and let God do everything for us" rest.

NO, SABBATH REST IS FURIOUS REST.

It's the kind of rest that powers our journey as we follow Christ with every ounce of our energy.

Consider the life of Paul. In the days after Christ's resurrection and ascension, Paul was a hater of the Christian message and perhaps the number one persecutor of the early church. He was on the fast track in the religious system of the day, with all the right credentials, education, and family ties. But a funny thing happened on his way to work one day. As Paul headed to a town called Damascus to oppress the followers of The Way, he met Jesus. Blinded by a bright light, Paul went from being a Christ-persecutor to a Christ-follower in one life-rearranging encounter.

As it turns out, Paul would be God's choice to be the driving force behind the expansion of Christianity throughout the known world. Reading the rest of the story in the book of Acts, there's no doubt Paul was a type-A personality. He was the sort who got things done, moving at a pace that would drop most of us in a matter of days. And on top of that, Paul faced physical hardship and persecution at every turn. But he never quit. In fact, he never even took his foot off the gas.

But Paul understood furious rest, penning the words "Christ in you, the hope of glory."[24] He knew the secret of

Christ's life within, a powerful engine of unstoppable strength that was greater than anything he could do on his own. That's why he goes on to write, "For this purpose also I labor, striving according to His power, which mightily works within me."[25] Paul knew that rest and labor were not mutually exclusive and he had no problem straining and striving to accomplish his mission. But Paul made it clear where the power came from.

That's what I call furious rest—giving all we have for the sake of God's fame, yet carrying Sabbath rest as we go, knowing that His life within us enables us to accomplish what He has called us to do.

Well, the meeting that day in Alabama went well. I now count those two business leaders as friends. For the better part of four years, we've been partnering to create music that will open people's eyes to the amazing Story of God that's going on all around them.

Not too long after that initial meeting, our team at Passion settled on the label name sixsteps (inspired by the story of King David's attempts to return the Ark of the Covenant to Jerusalem—read about it in 2 Samuel 6:12–15). Then we set out to create a logo. We landed on a design comprised of six little dots in a spiral, tiny elliptical shapes that get progressively smaller. The idea behind the dots was to brand our identity with a constant reminder

THAT HE MUST GET BIGGER

and we must get smaller.

The way we figure it, the world doesn't need more stars—that is, not if the story we are a part of already has one. So if there really is just one Star, our challenge is not so much to shun the spotlight as it is to redirect any bright light that comes our way onto Him. Success would mean people loving Him more than any of us, clamoring for His touch more than ours.

That kind of thinking came in handy a few months back when sixsteps released a Passion CD called *Sacred Revolution*. Recorded live at OneDay '03, a solemn day of prayer and worship that united over 20,000 college students in a field east of Sherman, Texas, the CD featured the songs of some of today's best known lead-worshipers.

In an effort to let buyers know what was inside, we

placed a sticker on the cellophane wrapper telling them what to expect within. Such stickers are fairly common on the CDs you buy, little marketing voices saying, "Hey, look over here, I have the hit radio single you love on me." Well, we wanted people to know why this disc was a must-have, so the sticker read, "New songs from David Crowder Band, Chris Tomin, Charlie Hall, Matt Redman, and others." That's exactly how the sticker read.

Did you notice name number two?

As soon as I saw the first copy on a store shelf, I thought I was going to have a mini-meltdown. I thought to myself, *Who's that? I mean, I've heard of Charlie Hall. But, Chris Tomin? Who is Chris Tomin?*

Chris *Tomlin,* I've heard of. But Chris *Tomin?*

Okay, so I understood immediately that it was a typo. Trust me, everyone on our sixsteps team strives for excellence, but how could we misspell the name of one of the four guys on our label? I mean, it's Chris Tomlin for crying out loud!

And then it hit me.

Actually, that's what sixsteps is all about—less of us and more of Jesus. The sticker was just affirming that direction—less of us, one letter at a time. Maybe somewhere down the road we'll get to the place where a sticker boasts, "New music from Pass," or "Great new songs from id Cro, arlie Hall, and Matt man."

What about a sticker that simply reads, "Jesus inside"?

I think the more we happily point to Jesus, the more we know that Sabbath rest has taken root in our hearts. That's why Sabbath rest (and the weekly embracing of a day to consider again just how great God is) is true and uncorrupted worship at its best. I have heard it said that, "Waiting on God ascribes to God the glory of being all to us." For when we tirelessly toil, as though that's what it takes to keep our ship afloat, we steal God's glory, elevating ourselves as sole providers and sustainers of all we have and are. By refusing to slow down and bring things to a halt we are telling God that He is not enough for us. Oh sure, we may sing the songs of praise and tip our hats in His direction, but our failure to remember the Sabbath is nothing more than foolish pride, arrogance gone wild, and mistrust unfurled—the very opposite of what worship is all about.

That's why worship and Sabbath go together. By ceasing from our efforts when God asks us to, we make much of Him. When we trust Him by resting in Him, we exalt the

Lord, championing Him as all-powerful in our purpose-ful inactivity.

Furious rest, you see, is not about doing nothing. It's about doing everything we do with the quiet confidence that our lives, families, businesses, ministries, relation-ships, and dreams are in His hands.

Maybe for you the circumstances are different, yet the weight is the same. You know, the weight of trying to make yourself out to be bigger than you are—of trying to figure out how to run your life on your own, of always trying to determine the outcome, control the relationship, close the deal, run the show, hold it all together, know the future, protect your interest, build your kingdom—the weight of playing the role of God in your life and the lives of those around you.

But be encouraged. Today is the Sabbath. Oh, it may not literally be Sunday, but Sabbath is a state of mind and attitude of the heart. Sabbath happens anywhere and every-where we let go of the controls and lay the cares of our lives at His feet.

So where is your future right now? Where is the out-come of your pressing dilemma? Is it in your hands? Is it in the hands of the businessman or woman on the other side of the table? Is it in the hands of a boyfriend or girl-friend? In the hands of a team of doctors?

Or is your life, and all that concerns you, in the hands of the God who constructed the universe effortlessly in one week?

If you want more rest and less "stressed," declare this very moment to be your Sabbath—the place where you pry your fingers off of the circumstances and people you are trying so desperately to control, the place you discover that life really does work better in His hands instead of yours.

EMBRACING smallness

God put Sabbath

in every week for a reason. And the looking up we do on that first day of the week must bear fruit in all the moments of every other day for us to stay connected to the reality of *I am not, but I know I AM.*

It's a small thing, but for the past few years the screen saver on my cell phone has read *"iamnot."* It's a subtle, but constant, reminder of the freedom I have found in being small, a reminder I need much more than I'd like to admit.

For me, embracing smallness is not a one-time proposition, but a daily event. That's why in Eden there wasn't one big Sabbath to end all Sabbaths. God knew how strong the undertow of sinful pride would be. He knew how quickly we would read and believe our own press. That's why a seventh day of rest has anchored each week from the beginning of time, and why Sabbath is still calling us to the end of ourselves today.

I have found that I can easily say (and teach) "*I am not but I know I AM*" all day long, but words are cheap and life is hard. Sure, the fruit of this "little me, huge God" truth is amazing. Who wouldn't want a life marked by "glorious death" and "furious rest"? But to mean it when I say that I want my life to count for His glory is to drive a stake through the heart of self—a painful and determined dying to me that must be a part of every day I live. That's what Paul was getting at when he said, "I die every day."[26] He was declaring his intention to come to the end of himself before he came to the end of his life—to die to self-power and self-glory long before they put his body in the grave.

If there's one thing we can all be sure of in our quest to live for His glory and His fame, it's that the flesh will not die quietly. No, our mortal selves will scrap and claw for every ounce of self-promotion they can get their hands on.

Whenever an opportunity presents itself, the voice of pride will rise up with a roar, urging us to take control. Whenever a spotlight is near, our flesh will run toward it and attempt to soak it in. That's why, like Paul, we must carry around an attitude of death everywhere we go, a moment-by-moment willingness to abandon the self-life—to let it die—no matter what the cost.

Humility, another word for knowing my name is *I am not,* can be described as "seeing God as He is."

> Pride is simply an admission that I haven't seen **GOD** at all.

Humility is the instant rightsizing of me that occurs with just one eyeful of His majesty. True humility (not the false kind that ends up being about us at the end of the day) is not a sign of weakness, failure, or inability, but rather a sign that we are getting to know God and have glimpsed His glory. And once we see how glorious His glory really is, we realize that all other glory is futile and fading, and totally inconsequential in the grand scheme of things.

One thing that's helped me look up this past year has been a book titled *The Universe: 365 Days.*[27] Based on the same premise as the picture-of-the-day website that NASA hosts, the book is comprised of a calendar and a cosmic photograph for each corresponding day. I have used it as a part of my daily approach to God for almost a year. Every now and then there's a picture of an astronaut or space-craft, but I skip over the celebration of what man has made and go right to the good stuff—the truly mind-stretching stuff of heaven that literally stops me in my tracks. On more than one occasion I've had to close the book and put it down because my brain simply couldn't compute the immensity and complexity of what I was seeing.

Say you didn't want to take the full 365-day journey, you could just check out September 23. The accompany-ing photo and text show our sun, a raging ball of fire, as it rocks our solar system with heat and light, converting its mass into energy at a staggering rate equivalent to 92 bil-lion nuclear bombs exploding every second.

Or flip back to January 14, where you'll find the Ring Nebula. This gaseous ring (a collection of dust and gas) is positioned in such a way as to allow us to look straight down its barrel and through to the other side. The hot gases toward the inside are a cobalt blue, cooling to fantastic hues of green, yellow, and red as they expand to the ring's farthest edges. The photo shows a tiny white dot in the open center. This dying star is emitting the gas that forms the massive and mesmerizing tie-dyed ring of the Ring Nebula (and inspired for me the phrase "glorious death").

Or check out October 4. There you'll find my personal favorite, NGC 628, "The Perfect Spiral Galaxy," a picture-perfect marvel containing hundreds of billions of stars floating through space 30 million light years away from earth.

You get the idea, right? Simply looking up into God's heavens seems to shrink whatever my day holds to a more manageable size...and remind me once again of His.

But, it's not just the expanse of the cosmos that helps me remember my smallness and God's bigness every day.

Really old things make me feel small. Like the pyramids. Or the Sistine Chapel. Or when I consider that hundreds of generations have passed before me and not a single person among them ever knew my name.

Mysterious things make me feel small, too. Mysteries like conception and the sovereignty of God.

Like eternity.

And often the tiniest of things make me feel smaller still, things like the sub-particles of sub-particles that make up the intricate building blocks of the matter that forms earth. Like the stuff of Nanotechnology, an area of science dealing with real world applications of activities at the level of atoms and molecules. These guys are dealing with small, *really small*. As it turns out, a nanometer is one billionth of a meter (a meter is about the length of your arm), or about one eighty-thousandth the diameter of a human hair. Somehow, knowing that people are measuring things in nanometers, and actually constructing useful things that are tens of thousands of times thinner than one of my hairs, makes me feel...infinitesimal.

That's what you are, and I am...infinitesimal.

Tiny bundles of nanometer-sized components, yet people **INFINITELY** loved by God.

When you get right down to it, trading in the little story of me is not really all that big of a sacrifice after all. Who wouldn't want to abandon a script you could fit on the pointed end of a pin for a chance to get in on the glorious epic that is so enduring that its screening will require all of eternity. Glimpsing His glory makes me want to say, "Your name and renown are the desire of [my soul]."[28] Seeing His true fame makes me want to live for a bigger purpose, doing everything I do in such a way as to shine the spotlight on Him.

But how do I do that on a daily basis? How do I live for His name in the daily grind?

Well, the answer is not easy, but it is simple—you do whatever it is you do in such a way as to reflect His character to the world around you. You don't have to be a preacher like John or Paul, or a missionary, or a worship leader, a Christian record label-type, or a church worker. In fact, you may even have a better shot at amplifying His glory if you're *not* any of those things. Everyone expects pastors and ministry-types to live for a bigger story, but how cool is it when people in every walk of life do what they do with a greater purpose in mind?

That's why Paul writes, "And *whatever you do*, whether in word or deed, do it all in the name of the Lord Jesus, giving thanks to God the Father through him."[29]

Paul is saying that living for God's glory is not so much about *what* you do as it is about doing *whatever* you do in such a way that it reflects Jesus Christ to those around you and ultimately points people to Him. In other words, you don't have a better chance of glorifying God by being a preacher than you do by being a bond trader, or by being a missionary verses being a mother. You don't get more credit in the kingdom of God for being a songwriter than you do for being a student.

And what does that kind of Christ-exalting life look like? For starters, being the best at what we do, leading in every strata of society, being honorable and dependable, walking with humility, and treating everyone we encounter along the way the same way Jesus would.

And how would we know when we have slipped back into the story of us? We know when we see these telling signs:

When I live like I'm privileged, I have lost the plot. In other words, when I start acting like I deserve a certain outcome or a higher standard of life, I have failed to strike the fatal blow to self and am living like I actually have rights in this world apart from God.

When I am demanding, I have lost the plot, insisting that God and others meet my needs on the timetable that I see fit.

When I act pompous, I have lost the plot, thinking that I am somebody while only proving that I haven't had a good look at God today.

When I crumble under the pressure, I have lost the plot, declaring that the outcome of life rests squarely on my shoulders, not His.

When I start protecting, I have lost the plot, marking turf as though it were actually mine and forgetting that everything I have comes first from above.

When I crave the spotlight for myself, I have lost the plot, losing sight of the story line and the one true Star.

And every time I do it I waste one of life's fleeting chances to make my life truly count by amplifying Him.

When I fail to celebrate the successes of others who are living for His fame, I have lost the plot, thinking that possibly we are on different teams when we actually share supporting roles in the same story.

When I dwell on feelings of being unloved, unnoticed, or insignificant, I have lost the plot, abandoning the miracle of knowing God on a first-name basis.

All of these privileged, demanding, arrogant, frazzled, turf-protecting, glory-stealing, self-loathing moments are nothing more than a clarion call alerting us to the fact that it's time to die again, reminders that the life of smallness requires a vigilant watch and a constant willingness to strike the fatal blow in the heart of me.

But to die to self is to gain on an unfathomable scale—
a daily funeral that is nothing more than the doorway to a life filled with the matchless

WONDER OF ALL THAT HE IS.

Jesus Christ—the great *I AM* come to earth—understood this well, being willing to shed His heavenly glory for a spot in God's redemptive story. He was willing to fully give of Himself so that ultimate glory could come to His Father.

Because He knew there was a greater glory to come, Jesus was never petty, pompous, demanding, or defeated—no matter what circumstance He faced. Just the opposite, He kept giving away Himself so that others (including you and me) could taste true greatness in a relationship with God.

Thus, Jesus defines a Christ-follower (Christian) as the one who models His lifestyle, one who will "deny himself, take up his cross daily and follow" Him.[30] He, too, knew that embracing smallness and crucifying the flesh is something we must do every single day.

That's why the ultimate expression of smallness is the death of self. It's the ultimate end that comes after the prayer,

"Less of me

AND MORE OF GOD."

To be honest, looking up doesn't make life's challenges and problems go away. Yet gazing into heaven reassures me that God still is *I AM*, and that His greatness, goodness, and God-ness is the best lens through which to view every day of my life.

you can TRUST HIM

Just because we agree that God is bigger than our ability to comprehend doesn't mean that we will automatically love and trust Him. And many, even among Christ's followers, don't. Not really. They don't trust His intentions, His reliability, His sensitivity to their needs, His timing. As you'd expect, then, they're reluctant to let go of their own story—no matter how small, self-focused, or unrewarding—to be a part of His.

Our trust in another person has to start somewhere other than in that person's size and strength. It starts in their proven character over time.

But you and I can trust our God with our lives for that very reason. God is not only big enough to make the universe; He has created a universe that is breathtakingly beautiful, intricately ordered, scientifically dependable, the stuff of architectural genius. The universe itself declares to us that God is beauty personified, that He is organized and detail-oriented, that He is reliable and trustworthy, that He is genius defined. It's not just that God made the world that causes us to trust Him—it's the *kind* of world He made.

Because He is good we can gladly resign our lives to His. Because of His character we can feel secure in His massive hands.

Still, sooner or later you and I will come to a crossroad—a crisis of trust, when the sky turns black and life seems to spin out of control. That's what happened to our friend John the Baptist not long after his encounter with Jesus at the Jordan River.

John's outspoken criticism of King Herod's marriage to his brother's wife did not sit well with the king or his new wife. So the king had John arrested and thrown in prison.

While John wasted away wondering when or if he'd ever be released, he heard glowing stories of the miracles Jesus was performing, and of the large crowds that followed Him everywhere. Time passed. John waited. Finally, John asked two of his followers to take a question to Jesus: "Are you the one who was to come, or should we expect someone else?"[31]

What John really wanted to know was: *If You are who I think You are, then why am I stuck in this jail? Why don't You come and perform one of Your miracles for me?*

We've all been there, wondering if God really is who we think He is—and if He is why He doesn't come and change our circumstances.

And what happened for John? Jesus sent a reply: "The blind receive sight, the lame walk, those who have leprosy are cured, the deaf hear, the dead are raised, and the good news is preached to the poor." All signs pointed to the fact that Jesus *was* in fact who John thought He was. But for reasons beyond our understanding, Jesus did not perform a miracle for John. He didn't even visit his prison cell.

And then for John, the worst happened. During Herod's birthday bash, the order was given for John to be beheaded—a senseless murder at the whim of the king's stepdaughter.

You'd think that if God was going to come through for anybody, He'd come through for John the Baptist. But He didn't. In fact, from where we're sitting it looks like Jesus let John down completely, standing by doing nothing while evil, cruel people took his life.

But think about this:

If John had lived a little longer he would have seen an even more senseless event than his own beheading. He would have witnessed the unthinkable—the "Lamb of God" being crucified at the hands of an angry mob. And for this cruel killing, John would also have concluded that God stood by and did nothing.

Yet God was very much at work, accomplishing something bigger than John or any one of us could ever imagine. The death of Jesus on the cross in what appeared to be a senseless murder was actually divine intervention. When it seemed that God wasn't powerful enough (or big enough) to stop the chaos, God was actually being both big enough and good enough to orchestrate our redemption through the sacrificial death of His only Son. Never before had the world seen love like this. God came down to do the dirty work of buying back our lost and doomed souls in the most staggering act of grace and mercy ever known.

I hope you see it clearly today: the cross of Christ is the place where trust in God is born. The death and resurrection of Jesus Christ is an act of kindness from a loving and trustworthy God, an undeniable demonstration of His goodness that we can cling to when our sight and understanding fail to make sense of the circumstances that surround us.

The skies declare that *I AM* is huge; but Calvary affirms that *I AM* has the best interest of every *I am not* in mind at all times. Our God is in the heavens and the whole world is under His command, but now because of Christ we can personally know how much He loves us and believe that He is using everything that comes our way for His glory and for our ultimate good.

Now you understand why I can so confidently urge you to exchange the starring role in your small story for a supporting role in our God's epic adventure. It's time for you and me to live as those who can never be the same because we have encountered both the great power and the great love of *I AM*.

And in the days to come, when you're questioning, needing, searching, wondering, asking, and struggling, you will find His sufficiency at the end of every desperate prayer. When you cry out all the things that you are not, you'll know His answer is, "I AM."

For every cry, there is one answer:

I need help.

I AM.

I need hope.
I AM.

Who could possibly be smart enough to figure this out?
I AM.

What works?
I AM.

What lasts?
I AM.

What's the latest thing?
I AM.

What's the hippest thing?
I AM.

I need a fresh start.
I AM.

I need a bigger story.
I AM.

My vision is bigger than my resources.
I AM.

Nothing's real anymore.
I AM.

Who can I trust?
I AM.

I'm not sure who's on my team.
I AM.

Nobody's listening to me.
I AM.

I don't have a prayer.
I AM.

My marriage is sinking and I don't know where to turn.
I AM.

I can't hold on.
I AM.

My kids deserve more.
I AM.

I'm pouring into others, who's pouring into me?
I AM.

If we fail, who will get the job done?
I AM.

I'm not sure why I'm here.
I AM.

I've given all I can give and it's not enough.
I AM.

I'm tired.
I AM.

I quit!
I AM.

I can't!
I AM.

I need a drink.
I AM.

I need a fix.
I AM.

I need a lover.
I AM.

Somebody just hold me.
I AM.

And what does this great I AM say of Himself? He says to you and to me: "I am the way, I am the truth, and I am the life. I am the resurrection and the life. I am Savior. I am Jesus—the solution, the restorer, the builder, the answer, the Wise One, the Coming One, the Mighty One. I am the Lord and there is no other. I am God and there is none besides Me. I am the First and the Last. I am Alpha and Omega. I am the Beginning and the End. I am the Lord, that is My name, and I will not give My glory to another, or any of My praise to idols. I AM THAT I AM, and that is My name—My memorial name to every single generation."

the
one-word
BIBLE STUDY
METHOD

The One-Word Bible Study Method (OBSM) isn't an official name, just one I have created for myself. Given that much of chapter 4 is built around the OBSM, it might be a good idea to talk through what the method is about and how it works.

A long time ago, through a seminary friend, I encountered the discipline of observation, or looking intently at a given object over an unusually long period of time. The approach is based on the famous teaching method of Louis Agassiz, a scientist who taught at Harvard during the nineteenth century. He regularly asked his students to look carefully at a fish (a preserved lab specimen), then write down a description of what they saw. When students thought they had noticed everything, they'd report their findings to the professor. But he would say, "No, no! You haven't seen it yet! Start over!" and send them back to study the fish again. This process of observing, writing down findings, reporting—and starting over again—would often last every day, all day, for more than a week.

Here's the thing: With each commitment to further observation, Agassiz's students made fresh discoveries— layer upon layer of greater detail, and deeper and more important insights than they would have ever noticed the first few times through.

Applied to the study of Scripture, the discipline of observation means that we look intently into the text for an extended period of time, waiting for the text to begin to breathe and disclose its meaning. Too often we speed read through the text, underline a key phrase here or there, and move on without giving the living Word enough time to take root in our hearts and reveal more of what it's about. But Paul writes, "Let the word of Christ dwell in you richly as you teach and admonish one another with all wisdom, and as you sing psalms, hymns and spiritual songs with gratitude in your hearts to God."[32] If we are going to know God well, and walk in intimate fellowship with Him, we have to immerse ourselves in His Word. It is the living expression of who He is to you and me.

In a sense, the OBSM is nothing more than meditation—allowing God's Word to slowly soak into our minds and hearts. The OBSM is *not* a substitute for conventional Bible study methods (exegesis). I'm not even saying that the OBSM should be your primary Scripture study path. But after you've applied a more traditional study approach (for example, an inductive Bible study, where you ask of the passage: "What does it say? What does it mean? and, How do those two things connect with my life?"), I think you'll find the OBSM extremely helpful for getting even more out of the text.

The OBSM works better with some types of literature than others. The history books, the prophets, and the narratives found primarily in the four Gospels don't usually work as well as the epistles (the bulk of New Testament teaching books), where the content is presented in logical sequence.

Take for example the book of Romans. Beginning in chapter I, verse I, the OBSM caused me to stop and park for a while on the very first word, *Paul*, where otherwise I would have probably kept on reading. Sure, it's just a name. But using the OBSM, *Paul* has become a one-word summary of the entire book of Romans. Why? In a sense all of Romans is depicted by the life story of this man, a hater of Christians and a persecutor of the church who was changed by God's sovereign grace from Saul into Paul, the writer of much of the New Testament and the first century's most effective mouthpiece for the gospel.

Every word in your study may not be spectacular, but many will, making the whole process worthwhile. As you find a verse or phrase you want to focus on and absorb, write it down on something you can carry with you. Read the passage one word at a time. Focus on each word until it starts talking back to you. After a while, you will probably see things you may have missed many times before. Patience is the key. You can't rush the process and you can't make the words tell you what you want to hear. Listen to them, and let your knowledge of all Scripture speak into what you're discovering in this particular passage.

I would have never observed *BE* in *beloved* or in *became* if I hadn't spent a lot of time wrapping my mind around the idea that God's *I AM* name also translates as *BE*.

why the
Beatitudes
are the
BE ATTITUDES

My use of *Be* as a personal devotional idea has helped open up other larger scriptural themes for me as I've studied verses in context. But, right off the bat, it's important to acknowledge its limitations.

For example, I understand that the use of the letters "be" in front of another word (as in the case of "became") to imply *I AM* is a personal interpretation, not a meaning inherent in the word itself. After all, *be* as a prefix has at least a dozen different meanings in its various verb formations in English, and many *be* combinations have no devotional implications at all. (I'm also aware that my personal interpretations get lost entirely when *be* words are translated into other languages.)

But if you're an English-speaker and are up for it, consider:

A few years ago I was speaking at a conference for teens. After one of the main sessions, a high school student came up to talk with me. She was a pretty typical sixteen-year-old, jeans, flip-flops, a couple of layers of tees and tanks, and a small corduroy shoulder bag slung low below her waist with a wide strap that she tugged on with her left hand. A couple of small button pins dotted the shoulder strap, one of which she was now detaching and holding in her hand as a four-foot-wide smile crossed her face and welling tears suspended in her eyes.

About the size of a quarter, the bright red pin boasted in bold upper-case letters, "I AM LOVED."

Anticipating her words, I reached out and took hold of the pin. "I just wanted you to have this," she said. "It's what you talked about tonight during the message. Thank you for reminding me how much God loves me and cares about me. I'm going through some really hard stuff in my life right now and I really needed to hear that again tonight."

Beautiful!

In that session we had been digging into the first three verses of I John 3. Even though most of the kids at the camp were using the New International Version of the Bible (the NIV is a very readable translation, phrased with language that reflects the idioms of modern culture), I had been teaching from the NASB. I am somewhat attached to the *New American Standard Bible* because I used it in the formative years of college, seminary, and beyond, and because the word sequence and word choices are truer to the original text in many instances than the NIV. On this night teaching from I John, I wanted the NASB word choice because it made this passage come alive in a much better light.

The chapter begins with this stunning proposition: "See how great a love the Father has bestowed on us, that we would be called children of God; and such we are."[33] And continues, "Beloved, now we are children of God."

Granted, *beloved* sounds a little "churchy," and it's not a word we use in our culture except at weddings and funerals. That's why the NIV has substituted the words, *dear friends*. But, *dear friends* doesn't work so well for me if the alternative is *beloved*. I'll take *beloved* any day!

And you should, too.

Beloved, as you know by now, is a compound word made up of the two words *be* and *loved*. *BE*, as we have already discovered, equals *I AM*. Thus, *beloved* translates: *I AM* loved. And that's who we are. You and I are *BE* loved.

That night we talked about how the word *beloved* could be used as a statement of fact, as in: "You are beloved (*I AM loved*) right now whether you feel it or think you deserve it. Right now, because of what God has done through Christ, you are beloved."

But we also talked about how *beloved* is a command, as in, "Be loved!" In this sense, God is the first mover and He is not really asking us to allow Him to love us as much as He is telling us to receive what He has already demonstrated in the death of His Son.

Well, this girl got it that night. Imagine her surprise when she looked down and saw that "I AM LOVED" pin staring back at her, an affirmation of the message God was writing on her heart.

In a way, the whole story of the gospel and the Christian life can be told by a handful of *BE* words.

Beloved.

Became.

Beheld.

Behold.

Become.

Be still.

Even the Beatitudes are now the *BE* attitudes (the God attitudes or *I AM* attitudes), descriptors of what I can *become* when *I AM* is living in me.

GOD'S PASSION FOR GOD'S GLORY (and why God is not an egotist)

When God made the universe, His goal was not to make a habitat for man, but rather to make a statement about Himself. As He fashioned earth, God was not simply acting as man's interior (and exterior) designer, creating a global environment we all would really love and enjoy. He was thinking mostly about Himself.

When He initiated the first ocean wave and carved out earth's deepest canyons, forming the very dirt we call home, God intended that everything about it would point us back to Him. When He created the first man and woman, God wasn't obsessed with the glory of the human race, but with His own glory. And it's there, everywhere—mysteriously woven into our DNA, the image-stamp of the Creator, allowing us to share a unique intimacy with the Almighty and reflect His glory.

Everything God does, He does for His own glory. He approaches every decision with the question: "What will bring the most attention and honor to My name in this situation—what will most glorify Me and make Me look the very best?" And then He does whatever that is.

To put it another way, God is into God. He is highest in His own thoughts, foremost in His own affections. While it is true that God loves you—really, really treasures and prizes you—God's first and central love is Himself. God doesn't love anybody more than Himself, will exalt nothing above His own name, and does everything He does to the end of displaying His supremacy and unrivaled glory. That's why everything in all of Creation is singing His song in this moment, and why the terminal confession of every human who has ever lived will be, "that Jesus Christ is Lord." Why? The same verse tells us: "to the glory of God the Father."[34]

But if God does everything He does for His glory, does that make Him an egotist? Does the fact that He is bent on having all of Creation bow down and worship Him make Him the world's biggest megalomaniac?

Well, if by the question we mean, "Is God full of Himself?" the answer is a resounding "Yes." (Then again, if you are God, who else are you going to be full of?) But before we ask if God is an egotist, we need to back up and ask two more basic questions.

The first is simply, "Is God God?" By that I mean, is God the truest, purest, most potent, most beautiful being in existence? Is He the sole proprietor of the universe, the originator of all that is, unchanging, eternal, and all consuming?

If the answer is yes, that leads us to the second question: "Does God know who He is?" Does God know that He is supreme in every way—unmatched in glory, might, rule, and reign?

Well, if God doesn't know who He is then He, by default, is not God, because one of the prerequisites of being God is knowing all things, one of which would be that You are God. So to be God, and not know that You are God, would be the proof that You were not who You claimed to be.

When God says, "I am the LORD; that is my name! I will not give my glory to another or my praise to idols."[35] He is passing the test of being God, declaring that He knows full well who He is. God knows who He is and knows that He is God alone. He knows that He is supreme in eternity—something that we know, by the way, only because He told us—and is fully aware of the fact that nothing, and no one, holds any value greater than His. God knows that He is intrinsically more valuable than all the worth of the world combined, and then some. (Actually...*and then a lot.* God is not just a little more valuable than the combined value of everything else in the universe that has value. He is *infinitely* more valuable!)

In the end, all of this doesn't make God self-centered as much as it makes Him God-centered, something that He has to be, and honestly, I want Him to be.

Are you with me?

Okay. So if God is God, and He knows who He is, God must perpetually exalt Himself in all things. For if God failed to exalt Himself in every possible way, He would exalt something or someone else as central, someone or something that was not central at all. This would make God both unwise and unloving—unwise, because it would demonstrate that He didn't know what was best; unloving, because He would be allowing our attention and affection to be aimed toward something that was less than the very best. But since God encompasses all wisdom and is the source of pure love, He has no choice but to exalt Himself above all things.

If that approach sounds a little arrogant or egocentric, we have to remember who we're talking about. We're not talking about little finite creatures like you or me, but about the God of gods who is before all things. If I make myself out to be central, or seek to exalt myself above all things, claiming that I am first or best, in that moment I become an egotist because I am neither of those things. I am not God, and I know it. But when God orchestrates life in such a way as to spotlight His fame, He is being anything but arrogant. He is doing the most loving thing He can do. When He calls us to glorify Him—when He demands our complete and unadulterated worship—He is not being egotistical at all, rather He is simply being God. And He is doing the very best thing He could possibly do for us in that He is causing us to stake our claim on the most beautiful and glorious One in all Creation. When God makes His glory the center of all things and the center of our affections, He gives us Himself—the very best gift He could give us, and the ultimate expression of love.

God is committed to Himself more than anything.

And God is determined that the story will remain about Him, concluding with the unending applause of heaven. His purposed preoccupation with His glory is a river that no man can tame, a sovereign tide that makes the pride-filled current of Eden, destructively massive as it is, seem like a desert trickle after a brief shower. As He did with Pharaoh, God will even use the greatest pride in man to amplify His glory, insuring in the end that every life and every tongue affirms His fame.[36]

To joyfully choose to make our lives count for His renown is to join His cause and to get on board with what He is already doing with or without us. In so doing, we make sure our lives count for what matters most while enjoying for all time the very best God has to offer.

Which is Himself.

notes

1. What's even more transforming is the reality that because of the gift of the Holy Spirit, God is not only always with us, but also in us through the person of Jesus Christ.

2. In fact, the universe is so big, scientists even need measurements greater than the light year. For even greater distances they use a unit of distance known as a parsec, which equals 3.26 light years, or a little more than 13 trillion miles.

3. Psalm 33:6, 9.

4. Isaiah 40:22, 25–26.

5. Luke 4:14–21.

6. Genesis 11:3–4.

7. Philippians 2:5–11.

8. John 1:20.

9. John 1:21–27.

10. It is here (in John 1:29) that the New International Version translation fails us and I reach back for the trusted *New American Standard Bible* of my youth. The NIV inserts the word *Look,* a very fine verb and an appropriate thing to say when your desired end is to cause people to see something. But, the NASB's *Behold*— and, yes, I understand that we are talking about semantics, not exegesis—puts John's confession in a whole new light.

11. John 1:29, NASB.

12. John 1:30.

13. John 3:26.

14. John 3:27–28, italics mine.

15. John 3:29–30.

16. John 3:31.

17. Mt. Sinai is also known as Mt. Horeb, the place where Moses had his initial encounter with God at the burning bush.

18. Exodus 20:8–11, ESV.

19. Psalm 46:1, 7.

20. Psalm 46:10.

21. Genesis 1:1–2.

22. Genesis 1:3–5.

23. Colossians 1:27.

24. Colossians 1:27.

25. Colossians 1:29, NASB.

26. 1 Corinthians 15:31.

27. Robert J. Nemiroff and Jeffry T. Bonnell, *The Universe: 365 Days* (New York: Harry N. Abrams Publishers, 2003).

28. Isaiah 26:8.

29. Colossians 3:17, italics mine.

30. Luke 9:23.

31. Luke 7:20–22.

32. Colossians 3:16.

33. 1 John 3:1–2, NASB.

34. Philippians 2:11. Sadly, most people think this magnificent proclamation about the Suffering Servant and His ultimate rule and reign ends with the exclamation, "every knee should bow...and every tongue

confess that Jesus Christ is Lord." But the passage
actually proceeds on from there to the conclusion, "to
the glory of God the Father," underscoring that the end
of the life, death, resurrection, and eternal rule of
Christ has at its core the exaltation of God and His
glory.

35. Isaiah 42:8.

36. Notice Exodus 14:17–18. "I will harden the hearts of the
Egyptians so that they will go in [the sea] after them.
And I will gain glory through Pharaoh and all his army,
through his chariots and his horsemen. The Egyptians
will know that I am the LORD when I gain glory through
Pharaoh, his chariots and his horsemen."

Gratitude

The process of getting this message into written form has been a challenging journey. I'd like to thank Don Jacobson at Multnomah for an endless amount of patience and encouragement along the way, as well as my editor, David Kopp, who has provided valuable assistance from start to finish. I'm grateful to you both for your unique gifts and friendship, and to all at Multnomah for helping carry this message to people everywhere.

As well, I want to thank my heavenly Father, the originator of the *I am not, but I know I AM* idea. As I recall, I was somewhere in the middle of a talk on God's *I AM* name one night in Colorado Springs when the idea *my name is I am not* suddenly shot through my mind. I'm pretty sure it was God whispering to my heart, right smack in the midst of my message. Before the talk was over, I was sharing with the group of youth pastors what God had just shared with me. The words stuck in our hearts that night with a resounding thud; a simple, memorable phrase that was both convicting and reassuring at the same time.

I've shared a lot of messages over the years, but never has one been met with the response of *I am not, but I know I AM.* T-shirts have appeared everywhere and poems, songs, and life-changing stories have flooded my mail and e-mail boxes. In it all, it's helpful to say out loud that all good things (ideas) come first from above, God generously sharing Himself with little *I am nots* like me. Thank You Father, Son, and Spirit Divine.

Many people have spurred me on during this journey—assisting, offering insight, and sustaining the vision of this book with their prayers and encouragement.

Among others, I am grateful for my assistant Jennifer Hill, Carrie Allen and the staff at Passion, Benji Peck, Gabe Lyons, Stuart Hall, Matt Redman, Thomas Womack, Jennie Graves, and Terry Willits.

Shelley, I love you. You are the best thing that has ever happened to me. Everything I do ends up being better (not to mention, possible) because of you. You are my joy in the journey.

iamnot

For more information on Passion Conferences
visit

268generation.com

For more on Louie, and to hear a portion of the
I am not, but I know I AM message for a limited time,
visit

louiegiglio.com.

Great resources from **sixstepsrecords**

Matt Redman: Facedown

From the sweeping title track, "Facedown," to the pulsing anthems "Dancing Generation" and "Mission's Flame," *Facedown* is saturated with the core belief that all true worship is a response to God's matchless revelation.

Chris Tomlin: Arriving

Bringing with it fresh and energetic musicality, *Arriving* offers Godward anthems for the church around the globe, constantly engaging the listener with the expanse of God's grace and majesty. Featuring "Indescribable" and "Holy Is the Lord."

David Crowder Band: Illuminate

Musical fusion and creativity abound in this latest release. With amazing artistry, new songs unveil the marvelous light of life in unique and spacious songs of intimacy and wonder. Featuring "O Praise Him (All This for a King)" and "Stars."

Charlie Hall: On the Road to Beautiful

Raw emotion and honest prayers collide as Charlie delivers twelve vibrant songs echoing the reminder that though God is infinite, He longs to be intimately connected with each of us. Featuring "I Will Overcome" and "Sending."

Passion: Sacred Revolution *Songs from OneDay03*

Stamped with a sense of holy awe, this collection of songs from OneDay03 carries with it more than great new music, it conveys the bigness of God and the desperation of a generation running hard after Him.

www.sixstepsrecords.com

Everybody's Got Religion

Not everyone may frequent the church on the corner, but we each have a

place of worship. For some, it's the office. For others, the mirror.

However, to worship anything less than God robs both Him and us.

True worship happens when we bow at the foot of the cross, reeling to

comprehend how a holy God could chase us down with kindness and

redeem us from an eternity of futile gods. Our sense of worship increases

beyond church walls and the Sunday routine, and all of life becomes our

delighted response to God.

The Air I Breathe

ISBN: 1-59052-153-6   Price: $9.99